PRAISE FO

MW00619284

The powerful "secret sauce" in *Live As A Leader* is liberally spread throughout every chapter embedded in the rich stories of real people in real situations, making the insights, lessons, and tools the authors offer us come vibrantly alive. This is one book that will fill you up to the brim with "aha" moments that will stick to your bones *and* that you can immediately apply to your work and your life. A MUST-READ!

—Roxi Bahar Hewertson, CEO at Highland Consulting Group, Inc. and Executive Leadership Coach; Author of *Lead Like it Matters . . . Because It Does* and *Hire Right, Fire Right: A Leader's Guide To Finding And Keeping Your Best People*

Live As A Leader is an exceptional blend of leadership concepts, true-to-life experiences, and calls to action. Aleta, Nancy, and John's message to strike a balance of *Inspiration* and *Accountability* while leading others will resonate with leaders in any seat. A must read for new and experienced leaders alike.

—Ellen Ingram, Director of Human Resources at America's Service Line, LLC

Live As A Leader is not just any book. While reading it, I felt like I was attending an inspiring workshop. The chapter on Resolving Conflict would single-handedly justify the book. I immediately implemented the following tools in my organization: Recognizing Conflict Questionnaire and Mediation Meeting Planner. Buy it for your people leaders!

—Derek Deprey, Head of Employee Success and Director of Leadership Development at ETE Reman and Author of *SHIFT: Move from Frustrated to Fulfilled*

The Living As A Leader team has done it, giving you the opportunity in this book to transform your leadership mind and inspire you to lead with humility, respect, and servitude.

—Stephen LeGrand, CEO at Timberlyne

I am so impressed with how well Living As A Leader has integrated their years of real-world experience into this easy to read and comprehend book. Aleta, Nancy, and John have hit all the key points covering the invaluable leadership skills that we need today to succeed.

—Randall Troutman,
General Manager at Printpack Medical

As competition for talent heats up in today's market, effective leaders will become the distinct advantage for organizations to attract, develop, and retain great employees. Aleta, Nancy, and John's message is that if you are continuously open to becoming a better leader, you will inspire and uplift others.

—Chris Smith, EVP International and
Chief Brand Officer at Jockey International, Inc.

Live As A Leader provides a realistic roadmap for anyone that aspires to be an effective leader. Whether you are a formal or informal leader, you will benefit by applying the principles of real-life leadership presented throughout this book.

—Michael Draver, SVP and GM at LPI

Live As A Leader provides perspective to leaders that helps them see things from the employee's point of view. It follows that up with practical tools and tips to implement truly effective leadership. When applied, leaders will be able to inspire their teams while holding them accountable, which will ultimately lead to success.

—Christine A. Specht, CEO at Cousins Subs

In the book *Live As A Leader,* the chapters don't need to be read in any particular order but can be selected based on the curiosity, challenge, or need of the reader at any moment. The authors have shared vignettes of experiences from their clients over the past twenty-five years that are real and useful. I recommend this book to the thousands and thousands of alumnae, facilitators, and coaches affiliated with Living As A Leader to remind them of the magic they have in their toolkit and also to everyone else who leads people and wants to engage, motivate, and build a legacy of positive impact.

—Rosemary M. DiMonte, Founder and Principal at Red Rooster Consulting, Inc., Experts in Strategic Planning and Strengthening Leaders, Chicago, Illinois

No matter where you are on your leadership journey, *Live As A Leader* is full of guiding principles that will help you continue to grow, develop, and reach your full potential as a leader.

—Tim Peoples, Senior Vice President of Supply Operations at Wis-Pak, Inc.

In this book, the chapter "Coach, Don't Confront" will give you many powerful takeaways. Learn how you can give your team what they crave and bring out their very best. I have worked with Living As A Leader over the past fifteen years, and this book encapsulates the tools of their teachings. Believe me, this approach works.

—Gregg Weber, Plant President, RRD

Aleta, Nancy, and John's book about the importance of accountability and inspiration is a fantastic source of leadership information. It is also a great workbook to help you apply it in your life and on the job right away. This book will help you accomplish better results for yourself and your team!

—Cory Bouck, Regional Business Director–Asia/Pacific at Johnsonville Sausage, LLC and Author of *The Lens of Leadership: Being the Leader Others WANT to Follow*

Live As A Leader should be read on a yearly basis. It's an effective breakdown of our constant leadership challenges with timeless solutions.

—Bill Sager, Founding Partner at Carousel

Of all the wonderful concepts and exercises in *Live As A Leader*, the Box of Life exercise will be transformational for leaders. To be given the tool of looking at people from a different perspective due to their different life experiences can break down barriers. In the questions lie the answers!

—Phil Areddia, Vistage Chair and Former President and CEO

Living As A Leader was instrumental in developing our people leadership culture at the company I previously led. In this book, you'll find key elements of their great training program and competence boost that empowered our managers with hands-on leadership methods and helped us form a strong leadership team!

—Markus Rauchhaus, CEO at Nott Company

Live As A Leader is a call to action for leaders of all levels. Aleta, Nancy, and John have filled this book with practical, real-world examples and given us the tools to be impactful and inspirational leaders.

—Dana Berry, Director of HR and
Certified Leadership Coach at Intermatic

No organization, i.e., company, government, church, non-profit or family, can achieve their potential without leadership. *Live As A Leader* clearly and succinctly lays out what good leadership is, its impact, and how we can each move in that direction.

—Jim Long, Aspiring Leader, Husband, Father, Friend,
and CEO, Board Member and Partner
at Pebble Creek Partners, LLC

Working with Living As A Leader has taught me that maintaining strong leadership is a constant endeavor. Balancing accountability and inspiration, staying outward-facing, demonstrating appreciation, taking on hard conversations are daily events when done properly. *Live As A Leader* demonstrates the skills your organization will need to maintain an intentional commitment to excellence.

—Gene Guskowski,
Founding Principal at AG Architecture

If you are ready to embark upon your own leadership journey, take this book along as your guide. You can have no better travel companions than Aleta, Nancy, and John, who provide practical guidance and sound advice while allowing for plenty of exciting discoveries along the way.

—Kent Wrenn, HR Leader and Talent Developer

LIVE AS A LEADER

Inspiration and Tools to Transform
Yourself, Your Team, and Your Life

BY

ALETA NORRIS
NANCY LEWIS
JOHN RUTKIEWICZ

Published by Author Academy Elite
PO Box 43, Powell, OH 43065
www.AuthorAcademyElite.com

Library of Congress Control Number: 2021915505
ISBN: 978-1-64746-867-5 (paperback)
ISBN: 978-1-64746-868-2 (hardback)
ISBN: 978-1-64746-869-9 (ebook)

Available in paperback, hardback, e-book, and audiobook

Any Internet addresses (websites, blogs, etc.) and telephone numbers printed in this book are offered as a resource. They are not intended in any way to be or imply an endorsement by Author Academy Elite, nor does Author Academy Elite vouch for the content of these sites and numbers for the life of this book.

Some names and identifying details have been changed to protect the privacy of individuals.

DEDICATION

To the thousands of leaders we have worked with
over the past three decades.

For your willingness, humility, challenges,
drive, and desire to improve.

CONTENTS

INTRODUCTION:
THE LEADERSHIP GAP

Dave was an executive who, when he was bored, got up and walked out of meetings. No explanation. He just left, leaving behind those who prepped for these meetings bewildered and unsure of what they did wrong.

Marie was a plant manager in a small town who wanted to be a friend to all her employees. She planned happy hours and gave gifts to those who reported to her. She was beloved by her team—as a friend. At the same time, her team stagnated, struggled to deliver results, and failed to live up to their potential.

Mark was a CEO who never really knew what he was going to say to his team until the moment he opened his mouth. Then he let his instincts take over. Usually, his instincts told him to berate, belittle, and yell at those around him. He thought that was the way to motivate them.

Then there was James, who was usually good-natured and liked to joke with his employees. Smart and highly experienced, he had worked in his job for thirty years and had more knowledge about the facility where he worked than anyone else. And he knew it. He could be arrogant, refusing to listen to anyone else. And under pressure, he would commonly become quick-tempered, barking orders at those around him.

These are just a few of the corrosive behaviors from leaders we've encountered in our thirty years of work at Living As A Leader. None of these leaders are bad people, and in the moment, they all genuinely thought they were doing the right thing for themselves and their companies. We're pretty comfortable in saying they likely didn't know better.

They didn't realize that, in their own way, each of these people created toxic cultures. They held back their teams, and they failed to build strong foundations for high performance and personal and professional growth.

There are many ways for leaders to fail, from a lack of empathy to a failure to hold others accountable.

Too often, leaders fall into these negative behavioral patterns. It can continue this way for years, with people making excuses for the leaders, for the company accommodating and working around leadership weaknesses, and for employees feeling powerless to change the structure. On and on it goes until it finally reaches a breaking point for people or for the organization itself.

Does any of this sound like a situation you've found yourself in at work?

If you're like most employees, the above examples probably sound all too familiar. According to a Gallup survey, 60 percent of respondents had left jobs or considered leaving when they didn't like their direct supervisors.[1] Consider a few more of the statistics:

- Employees who feel their voice is heard at work are nearly five times (4.6X) more likely to feel empowered to perform their best work (Salesforce, 2017).

- Of America's full-time workers, only 35 percent are engaged (Gallup, 2019).

- 23 percent of workers said they would offer more ideas and solutions, and 21 percent reported they would be willing to work longer hours if they trusted their leaders (Trust Edge Leadership Institute, 2018).

These statistics support a startling fact: the majority of employees leave work every day feeling unsatisfied. Further, these statistics suggest that workers are more likely to be higher performers if they have better relationships with their leaders. The tragedy of poor leadership isn't just that it hurts the bottom line and holds down company profits. It's that it affects people and families.

Think about it. The impact of poor leadership goes beyond the time people leave work for the day. It extends to the dinner table, where families decompress and talk about their day.

> THE TRAGEDY OF POOR LEADERSHIP ISN'T JUST THAT IT HURTS THE BOTTOM LINE AND HOLDS DOWN COMPANY PROFITS. IT'S THAT IT AFFECTS PEOPLE AND FAMILIES.

Leaders have a choice. They can be the kind of leader that inspires and uplifts people to be their best selves—or they can be the kind of leader that makes people vent, get frustrated, and look for other opportunities.

The sad thing is, many ineffective leaders never see themselves as the negative kind of leader or witness the harm they cause. Usually, they were promoted into positions of leadership because they were talented, high-achieving individual contributors and knew what they were doing. They may have high technical skill, but they have no experience when it comes to guiding, inspiring, and directing people. They've always been accountable to themselves and their own output. Then when they encounter other people who aren't like them, they don't know how to react. They default to acting in what they think is the right way in their mind—not in a way others need. Leaders make the mistake of treating employees as friends (instead of holding them accountable) or berating and belittling them (thinking that's the best way to motivate everyone).

No one taught them how to be a leader.

So far, we've focused on the consequences of poor leadership because it is unfortunately so prevalent. But the flip side is that leadership can also be transformational. Leaders can take low-performing employees and build them up. They can harness the energy of motivated employees and help them take the business to greater levels of success in terms of growth, revenue, profitability, and overall performance.

We've seen that it can be done with the right training, framework, and diligence. It takes time and commitment to develop as a leader, just as it takes time and commitment to learn and grow technical skills. Just as someone can become more proficient at tasks on the job, they can grow in leadership skills like empathy, accountability, and listening.

Sometimes we get asked whether good leaders are born or made. And the answer is yes, to both. We're all born with unique talents and personality traits. Personality is largely fixed by the age of three. But after the age of three, you likely learned to do a lot more to further your goals, from feeding yourself to driving a car. The same is true of leadership. Even if leaders don't change who they are as a person, they can choose to incorporate new skills and behaviors that make them the best versions of themselves—and help others around them reach their full potential too.

In this book, we will explore the most effective techniques for developing yourself into a confident and competent leader by sharing much of what we have seen throughout our thirty-year careers. Each chapter shares pragmatic principles that organizations and leaders can put into practice in, let's say, the right way. You will learn from others' mistakes as well as from the successes that have happened when people learn to turn a weakness into a strength.

Before We Begin

We came across a statistic years ago that said more than 400 books are written on leadership every year. Leadership seems to be one of those mysterious facets of human existence that all of us keep trying to get our arms around. And likely, every book about leadership strives to define what leadership is. We're no different.

In our work with leaders across North America—who lead at every level within their organizations—we strive to remove some of the mystery of leadership by defining it simply as this:

Leadership is . . .
engaging other people
to deliver desired results.

This simple definition brings with it three important implications.

First, it states that there are essentially two key elements you need to be focused on and concerned with as a leader—people and results. Both are required for you to be an effective leader because they work in tandem.

The people side of leadership is a leadership responsibility we call Inspiration. How do you inspire, engage, and motivate people through your leadership in a way that they want to follow you? This is not about being charismatic or a social extrovert. This is about behavior. For example, how do you treat your people, communicate with them, coach, develop, and even discipline them? These behaviors and how you go about them all impact your team's willingness to follow you, and so they impact your ability to lead. Think of the classic description of the leader as a bus driver—if you don't take your people where they want to go, they'll get off the bus.

But where *do* we need to go? The results side is also important. It's a leadership responsibility we call Accountability. You and your team do your work within an organization; that organization expects you and your team members to deliver certain results. As the leader, then, you need to create the conditions for accountability to those results. So, how do you provide direction, set goals and expectations, explain the rationale for a change in priorities, and measure performance—so that your people always have a clear vision of what success looks like and the results they are responsible for achieving?

The real challenge in effective leadership comes from balancing these two elements—people (Inspiration) and results (Accountability). Sometimes it can feel like these two don't fit well together. For example, Joe on your team wants to work on his special project, but the business needs him to complete and publish his weekly reports. How do you redirect him to prioritize the reports? Marsha always exceeds her sales numbers, but she's rude to the support staff. How do you coach Marsha to shift her interpersonal behavior? Cheryl has always done great work and is a passionate member of the team, but lately, she's been missing deadlines and seems cold and distant. How do you address those factors with Cheryl to get her back on track and re-engaged?

Effective leadership entails blending and balancing these two seemingly contradictory elements—Accountability and Inspiration—in a way that your team gets great results and is energized to keep doing the work. Accountability and Inspiration are like two oars of a leadership rowboat. We need them both, and we need to be good at them both. Overemphasize just one, and you end up rowing in circles. But it can be done, this balance of Accountability and Inspiration, and we'll show you how.

The second implication in our definition of leadership is that leadership does not require you to have an anointed role or specific authority. Yes, we assume that, in reading this book, you lead of team of direct reports in an organization, whether yours is a team of front-line workers, volunteers, or VPs. So, you have the title (or aspire to have it), but a title isn't necessary for you to lead. Leadership extends well beyond your role or authority. There are plenty of people in your work world who you need to "engage to deliver desired results" even though they don't report to you. You lead and influence your peers, colleagues, vendors—even your own boss. You often need to get results *through* these other people, even though you have no formal authority over them.

In other words, you don't need to be a "manager" to be a leader. In fact, throughout this book, we use the term leader (over manager or supervisor) because we want to continually underscore that you can lead from any seat, wherever you are, at any time. Leadership encompasses certain skills and behaviors that can be applied and transferred between and among all the roles you play at work—and in life. The strategies, techniques, and behaviors we'll share with you for great leadership work well within all of your important relationships, even at home—with your spouse, significant other, children, friends, neighbors, on and on.

You can "live as a leader" wherever you are.

It's Not About You

The third and final implication in our definition of leadership is subtle—but it's the most important of the three.

When you're a leader, it's not about you.

Look again at our definition: "Leadership is engaging other people to deliver desired results." Nowhere in that definition is there a reference to you and your results. Yes, we get it: Every leader today is a "working leader." You have your own projects and deliverables you're responsible for, but those responsibilities are not your leadership. They are the ways you personally and directly contribute to outcomes. Your leadership is a separate and distinct way that you contribute to the success of the team and organization—components that are outside of and greater than you. Leadership is about enabling and enhancing the ability of others to be successful at delivering the results *they* are responsible for.

WHEN YOU'RE A LEADER, IT'S NOT ABOUT YOU.

Every failure of leadership we see comes, in some way, from the leader's overemphasis on *me*. For example, a leader who berates her team member for missing a deadline reacts out of her attachment to the result. She aligns herself to the result, taking it personally as if she and the result are one and the same. That attachment leads to her lashing out, which will probably disengage her team member further.

Or, take the leader who avoids coaching a team member who is underperforming because he, the leader, finds such conversations difficult and uncomfortable. He is failing to lead because of his own emotional discomfort, forgetting that his responsibility as a leader is to help the team member succeed. Without a conversation, failure will continue.

Successful leaders see their role as leader to be outward-facing, not inward-facing. When things go well, they give credit to the team. When things don't go well, they look for what they themselves did that prevented or impeded success, and they look for what they can do differently and productively to help the team get back on track.

Strong, successful leaders know that their own success comes only through fostering the success of others.

Are You Willing to Go on This Journey?

No change worth happening ever takes place overnight. If you want to finish a marathon, you won't transform into a distance runner after one run. And no leader became an inspirational force and accountability genius after one meeting with a direct report.

Developing good leadership takes time, dedication, and practice. First, we have to identify where we have opportunities to make a more positive impact as a leader; then, we need to be committed to developing new skills and behaving differently to improve our overall effectiveness.

So, on a scale from one to ten (ten being highest), answer for yourself these two questions:

How willing are you to be a more effective, competent, and confident leader? What's your number? Write it down here.

What's your current level of ability (skill level) as a competent and confident leader? Write down your number.

Like any other pursuit, your willingness to grow, develop, and change the way you lead will directly impact and propel your progress through this book. This journey will require effort and practice. Each chapter includes action steps and exercises to get you going. We encourage you to devote time and energy to these steps and actions and to practice them as many times as necessary until you feel comfortable and proficient. And even more important, continue these steps until you have helped your team transform.

If you're not willing to take this journey, or your willingness is very low, this book might be better for another time—or as a gift to someone else.

> YOUR WILLINGNESS TO GROW, DEVELOP, AND CHANGE THE WAY YOU LEAD WILL DIRECTLY IMPACT AND PROPEL YOUR PROGRESS THROUGH THIS BOOK.

As for your ability and skill level, that's a benchmark. It's an overall gut check to give you a gauge that you can measure again at the end. Undoubtedly, as you considered your ability number, you were aware of areas where your skill level is high and other areas where you struggle. That's ok. Use that knowledge and insight to pay attention to what resonates as you read on to identify what's most important for you. Effective leadership entails a common set of principles and practices, yet every leader is different and needs to develop and grow in different ways. Be aware of what you need most to become the best leader you can be.

The path to becoming an effective leader won't be easy. Nothing worthwhile ever is. But it can be done, and we know because we've seen it time and again.

Ready to begin?

Let's learn how to live as a leader.

1

SEEING PEOPLE AS PEOPLE

Tim had never seen such a disconnect between a leadership team and the rest of a company before. As a plant manager, Tim was brought in to turn around a culture of low morale and distrust at one of the world's largest fruit-processing facilities. The situation he found at this new plant created a divide between leaders and the rest of the plant—literally.

The corporate leadership team operated in a corporate office building a few blocks away from the rest of the plant. There was an informal rule—enforced through tradition if not on the books—that the leadership team parked in an unofficial executive lot. As a result, a wedge formed between these opposing camps as they grew apart.

"There was a lot of draconian behavior at that facility," Tim remembered.

Tim's first action at the new plant was to help bridge the physical and emotional gap. First, any employee who got to work first could park anywhere. Period. There was no such thing as an executive lot. Second, he moved corporate leaders over to the plant so they were visible and accessible to employees. He then regularly took the leadership team on

1

walks throughout the plant. He wanted workers and leaders to see each other on a regular basis.

As a symbol of goodwill, he then set up his own office in a communal conference room in the plant. He told his staff that if anyone had any issues they wanted to bring up, they could come in and talk to him anytime.

"If you happen to have a need," he told his team, "I will be sitting right here. I will make myself fully available to you."

Then he ran into another roadblock. The employee badges were restricted, and employees physically weren't allowed to access the office area that held Tim's conference room. So he called IT and told them to give employees access to offices during work hours.

"We are going to fix this, and we are going to fix it today," he announced. "All employees need to have access to the office areas. During normal business hours, they need to see me, and they need to see us."

Each rule, by itself, was not major. All workplaces need structure and regulations. But each small indignity or attempt to keep the workers in their place added up to a culture of opposing sides in the same company. This was not lost on the employees. In an online review, one employee wrote how corporate leaders seemed to work in their own bubble. Another employee noted the lack of teamwork between teams because of management practices pitting teams against each other. Somewhere along the way, this company stopped seeing people fully as people.

Over the years, we've talked with leaders about what it means to respect someone. It means to have regard for them: their preferences, concerns, ideas, opinions, dreams, hopes, and struggles. They have to matter. The word regard comes from the origin of the word guard: to watch over, defend, and take care. True leadership, at its core, has regard for others in all situations.

For Tim, this wasn't his first time being tapped to complete a turnaround, but this was his most challenging to date. We started partnering with Tim to equip him and his leaders with tools and techniques to help employees feel trusted, safe, and, above all, human. Put simply, their job was to treat people as people.

After physically opening up the workplace, Tim's next step was to get employees to open up and talk. He wanted to hear from as many people as possible. Instead of a traditional roundtable—which can be dominated by a couple of strong personalities—we recommended sessions with markers, flip charts, and sticky notes where everyone could write down their own thoughts and opinions and ask questions. The room full of thoughts, opinions, and questions made for great team discussion. Tim did this again and again, with around twenty small group sessions. Themes began to emerge. And more importantly, employees finally felt heard and respected.

"Everybody is now participating, and everyone has their voice heard," Tim remembered of these sessions. "Now we have a platform for conversation."

Tim is a tall and imposing man with a dark beard who looks like he could play linebacker. He's the kind of guy who looks like if he barked orders, others would jump and listen. But that belies a gentle demeanor—and one that's more effective. Tim's goal in this situation was not to come in telling people how things needed to be done—his way or the highway. Instead, it was to level the playing field, treat others with dignity, and open doors—sometimes literally open doors. Taken together, these simple but powerful steps helped create allies rather than competitors.

Creating allies, forging connections, and building relationships is the first step in leadership development. Before leaders can make change, increase profitability, and impact bottom-line results, they need to see and treat people as people.

> BEFORE LEADERS CAN
> MAKE CHANGE, INCREASE
> PROFITABILITY, AND IMPACT
> BOTTOM-LINE RESULTS, THEY
> NEED TO SEE AND TREAT
> PEOPLE AS PEOPLE.

That's how your team starts to share a common cause. That's how you create the conditions where your people want to follow you.

Becoming Other-Centered

When we begin working with a new group of leaders, one of the first things we tell them is what we told you in the introduction: When you become a leader, it's no longer about you. To lead effectively—to engage other people to deliver results—leaders need to transition from self-centeredness to other-centeredness. This is an essential shift. Sometimes with leaders, we're more direct, telling them: "Get over yourself!" Of course, we say it with a grain of salt, but for some people, it's the first time anyone has ever challenged them about the risk of being self-focused or self-centered as a leader.

Many new leaders, as well as those who are more seasoned, still think leadership is all about them: It's about their promotion, their raise, their title, their power, their corporate climb, their accomplishments, their awards, or their corner office. In fact, one leader said to his employees, "Listen, I want to get one thing perfectly clear; I don't work for you. You work for me." This person is missing the boat entirely.

When we work with leaders, we plant the seeds at the beginning. We tell them that as soon as they accepted the role as leader of other people, they willingly signed up and acknowledged that moving forward will not be about them; it will be about others. This means taking time to learn the role and responsibilities of a leader. It means having a plan for intentional, or designed, leadership. It is now about being able to put your employees, or your team, first. It is about being able to put your own work aside when necessary to talk with an employee, solve a problem, or help an employee without saying, "I'm really busy right now. Can't it wait until later?"

Not everyone is ready or able to give up self-centeredness and switch to other-centeredness at the same time in their life. There may be a need to resolve other areas of life before they can make such a shift. The American Psychology Association states that the average age at which a person shifts from being primarily self-centered to other-centered is thirty-eight. Their rationale is that during early adulthood, there's a self-centered focus on acquisition, accomplishments, and survival when earnings are less. This is a time when people are looking for their life partners, settling into the right company, striving for promotions, earning additional degrees, trying to pay bills, buying their first house, starting a family, and so forth.

As you are personally able to make the shift from self-centeredness to other-centeredness, you will be that much closer to being an effective leader. How can you tell? You will honestly feel good inside when an individual, or team, succeeds under your leadership. It's even simpler to tell that you have arrived as a leader when you walk into a room and recognize that it's not about these people being lucky you've arrived, but about you being grateful they are all here.

To get to this place, it helps if you shift and change the way you think about other people in two fundamental ways.

Everyone Has a Box of Life

In our own lives, we recognize how a variety of complex factors shape our actions. We know if we showed up late for an appointment, it could be because the baby needed a diaper change right before we walked out the door, or we hit traffic when a car accident closed down the freeway. But as we observe others, we only know what we see on the surface, and we make assumptions. If you were late, I might assume that it's because you can't stick to a schedule, you're lazy, or you don't view timeliness as a priority.

In psychology, this is called the Fundamental Attribution Error. This means that, for ourselves, we ascribe all the situations and environmental conditions that we know went into shaping our actions. But in others, we only see the surface, so we don't stop to think about everything they may be struggling with, thinking about, or facing. No one holds a sign around their neck that says, *I'm worried about my mother's health while she gets medical tests today, and that's why I seem distant at today's meeting.* Or, *I have a special needs child, and that is what makes my schedule less predictable than others.* Seeing someone check out at a meeting, we may think they're disengaged or just don't care about this project. Or working with someone who requires more flexibility in their schedule may feel unfair unless you realize the unseen challenges.

It takes time and effort to get at the true motivations of others. But like peeling an onion, there are always more layers than what you see on the surface.

One way to begin softening our very-human tendency toward Fundamental Attribution Error is a practice called *sonder*. You can practice right now, especially if you are in public. The idea of sonder refers to the profound feeling of realizing that everyone, including strangers you pass on the street, has a life as rich and complex as your own. Practice sonder on the street, the train, a coffee shop, or anywhere people are around.

Right now, for instance, we're in a coffee shop on a Saturday morning. An older man, perhaps in his late seventies, is sitting side by side with a man in his twenties with similar features, probably his grandson. The older man has close-cropped white hair, and the younger man has dark hair, tattoos, a trendy haircut, and new clothes. They come from different generations. They likely have a different vocabulary and value different things at distinct stages in their lives. But they are watching a soccer game together on a tablet in front of them. They both love soccer. Grandpa played professionally in Europe when he was younger, and some of his grandson's fondest memories from his own childhood were the times when Grandpa played soccer with him in the backyard, teaching him how to dribble and pass. And Grandpa attended every game his grandson played in middle school and high school. Today, they're coming together to watch Grandpa's old team in the championship. Soccer has been their common passion for bridging a divide of maybe forty or fifty years. They understand each other through it, and their bond runs deep.

Or at least that could be what we tell if we glimpse beneath the surface. Every person has a story.

Look at the people surrounding you right now or think about the people you saw on the street today or in the restaurant at lunch. Realize that they all have lived rich and full lives just like you, full of hardships and pain, hopes and dreams, love and heartbreak, with boring, mundane tasks and moments of pure joy. They all have perspectives on life and belief systems and goals for the future.

Now, you could pick any one of those people and, through sonder, imagine what their story is like, as we did with the two men in the coffee shop. Was the story we told ourselves about their lives and relationship correct? We'll never know! But that's not the point. The point is to open ourselves up to the realization that rich and complex possibilities exist in the lives of everyone we meet.

The same is true for the people you lead. Remember that we can see below the surface of our own actions, but we don't automatically think about the backstories that drive and shape the lives and actions of other people, including our employees. It takes an extra effort to see what's driving their attitudes, beliefs, and actions. For leaders, it's necessary to take an additional step and learn about the deeper motivations of your team.

In our practice, we call this the Box of Life exercise. Think about your own Box of Life. You have it with you wherever you go. And no one—not one person—has a box exactly like yours. Your box contains your experiences, lessons learned, your hopes and dreams, education, your upbringing, your innate tendencies, your values, and so much more. Your Box of Life shapes who you are and how you operate in the world. More important, it shapes how you *see* the world. It shapes your judgments and assumptions about the events going on around you. It shapes how you think the world and other people should be. If the event reflects what's in your box, it's right. If it's not in your box, it's wrong.

> YOUR BOX OF LIFE SHAPES WHO YOU ARE AND HOW YOU OPERATE IN THE WORLD.

Let's take an example. Suppose you have a new person on your team, Sandy. Over the course of the first few weeks with Sandy, you notice that he doesn't quite seem to finish things. He does everything to about 80 percent, then stops.

As Sandy's leader, how would you react and respond? If you're like most leaders we work with during this exercise, your reaction to this scenario might be that Sandy is lazy, he doesn't care, or he doesn't like the job. Like most leaders, you probably got to your leadership role in part because you pay attention to details, follow through to completion and have high standards for doing good work. Those ways of being are elements within your Box of Life. So what's up with Sandy?

The answer is: We don't know. The real question is, "What's in his Box of Life?" What is it that's going on for Sandy that you don't know or understand? Your assumptions that he is lazy or doesn't care or doesn't like his new job don't help. Your "stories" about Sandy's performance will likely only lead you to feel frustrated, impatient, or intolerant.

Could it be that Sandy is more of a big-picture thinker who doesn't tend to focus as much on details? Did you know that about a quarter of our population is wired that way? Could it be that Sandy believes that he is, indeed, taking his projects to the expected level of completion, based on the training he received when he joined your team? Could it be that his mind is elsewhere because his fiancée just broke up with him? These are sonder-like questions, and they're good questions, yet they only take us so far.

If you really want to create allies among the people you lead, if you really want to forge connections and build relationships with them—so you can engage and inspire and lead them—you'll need to get to know them as people. They are not furniture, robots, or machines. They're complex people, just like you. Learn to see and understand who they are.

Lead with Curiosity

When someone on your team does something you don't understand, or that frustrates you, get curious. Ask questions to understand what's going on for them.

We talked earlier about peeling the onion. This skill of peeling away the outer shell to get underneath can be learned and practiced. We practice this skill regularly with our clients. We pair together two concepts we refer to as "let them hold the ball" and "peel the onion." Put the ball in their court and let them take control, let them explain, let them tell their story. Then peel back the layers, one by one, through effective questioning. Remember to let *them* continue to hold the ball, do most of the talking.

Your confusion about someone's actions or behaviors can be a great source for questions. With Sandy, for example, you're confused about the fact that he seems to stop short on projects. What's that about? What's behind it? What is his level of understanding about what "done" looks like in the context of your team's work? What is his understanding of the expectation? It's OK to be confused. Let that confusion spur your curiosity.

Leading with curiosity brings two advantages. First, it helps you focus on something other than your own assumptions or emotional reactions. You make it a point to find out the rest of the story rather than make up your own. Second, such an approach, especially with your team members, gives you a chance to understand them better. As a result, it builds trust. The goal isn't to pry into their personal lives or deepest, darkest secrets. The goal is to learn what makes your people tick. The goal is to learn how each person on your team needs to be led. Each of them is different as a person, a human being. Your job is to understand each of them so you can tailor your leadership to what they need most from you to be successful and deliver the results you seek.

In Stephen Covey's classic book *The Seven Habits of Highly Effective People*, habit number five is: "Seek first to understand, then to be understood."[2] We believe this to be a fundamental practice of effective leadership. And so does Tim, whose story opened this chapter. His whole mission to reinvent the culture of his new company was based on understanding how people felt, what they had experienced, and what obstacles were in their way. He sought to understand them, involve them, and listen. You can too.

Reflection: The Box of Life

On the following page, think about your own experiences with others at work, whether they're members of your team, colleagues, or peers. Answer the questions there to reflect on this concept of the Box of Life.

All of the exercises in this book are included in a printable Resource Guide. You can find and download this Guide at www.livingasaleader.com/book.

The Box of Life

What are one or two recent examples when I've become frustrated or impatient when others don't do things "my way"?

Is it fair of me to think others should do things my way? Explain.

How will understanding the Box of Life help me to better lead others?

What is one opportunity I have right now to apply the Box of Life in an employee situation?

Everyone Wants to Feel Valued and Appreciated

We mentioned earlier that there are two ways to make the shift to other-centeredness. One is to remain aware, consciously and intentionally, that everyone has a Box of Life. Build the habits of asking questions and listening to understand other people, how they think, and how they see the situation at hand.

The other way to shift to other-centeredness is to realize that everyone wants to feel valued. On this topic, leaders may think that they're communicating their gratitude or appreciation for others. But the reality is, it may take more effort than you think to help others truly feel like they are appreciated.

The underlying issue starts with the brain and neurochemistry. When people receive or perceive criticism, their fight or flight defensiveness kicks in and produces a rush of cortisol, a hormone that shuts down the higher thinking part of our brains and activates protective behaviors. Have you ever stewed over criticism or what you thought was a slight? We all have. This brooding process then keeps producing more of the cortisol chemical and magnifies fear or anger even further, acting almost like a sustained-release pill of bitterness. The negative effects can last up to twenty-six hours. On the other hand, a compliment or positive conversation releases the feel-good bonding chemical oxytocin. The only problem? This positive chemical doesn't last as long as the defensive cortisol, as it is metabolized quicker in the brain. So, while praising others around you gives them a boost, one critical comment can quickly reverse the feeling and last much longer.[3]

This reality doesn't mean leaders should never provide constructive and critical feedback. Providing honest and helpful ways to correct behavior is necessary to being a leader. It also doesn't mean that leaders should wrap all of their critiques in fake compliments. It simply reminds us that leaders need to be mindful of the power of their words, especially the ratio of complaints to compliments. It takes a sustained effort of intentionally noticing the good and genuinely showing appreciation to make people feel valued.

We often work with groups of leaders who have, for the first time, been introduced to the importance of catching people doing things right. When leaders are physically present with their teams, they can see little things going as planned. They can also see the hard work employees put in day in and day out—and recognize their value. Over time, employees will stop looking over their shoulders and feeling nervous about a rebuke from a boss. Instead, they will welcome the attention of their leaders seeing and complimenting a job well done. This exercise also trains leaders to see their people as people, not just as corrections that need to be made.

We tell leaders to treat their employees like they are wearing a big neon flashing sign that says MMFI—*Make Me Feel Important!* No one wears a big neon flashing sign that says *Kick Me Kick Me Kick Me.* One group of leaders we worked with began to see a big difference in employees within weeks of practicing making people feel important: less complaining, more working, and even increased smiling.

> MMFI—*MAKE ME FEEL IMPORTANT!*

One shared, "An employee recently told me that the only time he ever hears from me or anyone is if he's done something wrong. He told me that no one ever tells him when he is doing something right. So, I've made it a point to acknowledge the positive things I see. He really appreciates it and feels better about coming to work." Another leader shared, "Kevin is a new supervisor in our plant. He's been here for two months, and at the end of every day, I see him thanking his guys for coming in to work. This is so different from the supervisor who preceded him. I can already see a difference in the positivity and work efforts of these guys."

Because leaders tend to be self-starting and self-motivated, they often don't need praise or recognition. Therefore, they don't think others need it, either. Again, their own Box of Life limits their actions. Leaders may have the opinion, "Why in the world would I thank people for coming in to work? That is what they get paid to do." But pay alone doesn't inspire higher motivation. Factors like salary, health insurance, and working conditions are what psychologists call "hygiene factors," or the basic requirements for someone to take a job and show up to work each day. In contrast, meaningful praise is transformational and elevates people's desire to do more on the job. If showing appreciation for the small things will make a difference, why not show that appreciation?

The benefit of praise is not just about generating feel-good emotions, though that outcome is certainly one focus. It's also about results. Up to 30 percent of a company's financial results are determined by the climate of the organization, according to emotional intelligence expert and author Daniel Goleman, who was cited in a *Harvard Business Review* article titled "Leadership that Gets Results." Goleman also concluded that up to 70 percent of an employee's perception of the organization's climate is attributable to the actions and behaviors of his or her direct leader. The leader creates the environment that determines the mood of followers and their level of engagement and productivity. The leaders model the behavior, and the rest of the team follows suit.[4]

In the area of recognizing their teams, most leaders are falling down on the job. The impact of this lack of recognition is significant. Employees who report that they're not adequately recognized at work are three times more likely to say they'll quit in the next year[5]—that's because there's a direct link between praise and being engaged. The fact is that numerous studies show that the better leaders engage their employees, the better the bottom line. For example, Kenexa Research

Institute WorkTrends™ Report found that the top 25 percent of corporations, as measured by employee engagement, saw a five-year total shareholder return of 18 percent. The bottom 25 percent of corporations, as measured by employee engagement, saw an approximately 4 percent negative return for the same period. More recent evidence shows even more compelling results. One study illustrated the impact of extraordinary leaders on the bottom line. Using their research, they divided leaders into three categories and found that the bottom 10 percent of leaders saw a net loss of $1.2 million, while the middle 80 percent of leaders saw a gain of $2.4 million. The top 10 percent of leaders saw $4.5 million in gains.[6]

Long story short, poor leaders lost money, good leaders made money, and extraordinary leaders more than doubled the company's profits. And it all started with treating employees like they're human, praising them when appropriate and recognizing their value.

Reflection: Who Needs Positive Feedback?

On the following page, take a few minutes to think about your team or others you work closely with. Isolate one person you can acknowledge for good work. Then, plan out a conversation using the notes provided and have the conversation.

Who Needs Positive Feedback?

1. Select an employee on your team (or someone you work with closely) who is overdue for some positive feedback from you.

2. How will you deliver the feedback (email, phone, handwritten note? Privately or publicly? "On the fly" or in a scheduled conversation)?

3. What specific examples will you cite about their effective behavior or performance?

4. What is the positive impact of their behavior or performance on the team, the organization, or customers?

5. What is a question you can ask to engage the person in conversation about their behavior or performance?

Seeing People as People

The next time we worked with Tim, he had moved on after twenty-three years with his last company to take a senior vice president role in a family-owned bottling company with multiple locations throughout the country. The corporate headquarters is located on the edge of a small town. Farm equipment dots the landscape as you drive to the plant. Tim's office is a modest room adjacent to the bottling lines. Behind his desk are bottles manufactured in the plant alongside leadership books. His chair looks out to a map that shows the locations of the company's plants spread out across the country.

In his new role, Tim called us in to meet with his senior leadership team and begin working with the leaders throughout the organization. They had been using the same practices for decades, but now there was added pressure as new trends disrupted the beverage industry. After fifty years in business, it was time to innovate, evolve, and compete—all to help ensure a successful next half-century.

The situation was different this time, but the techniques were the same. Tim didn't want to tell everyone how to do things his way. His first priorities were to get buy-in, meet his team, and build goodwill. One of his first steps was to schedule ongoing one-on-ones with his leaders. This was a new concept to many in the organization.

"When I first started scheduling these with people, they said, *'What are these?'*" Tim remembered. "For folks who aren't accustomed to them, they first think, *I'm in trouble.*"

This is a common reaction. At another company, someone dressed up for their first one-on-one, not sure if it was a performance review or a firing. The intention, again, isn't to catch people doing something wrong. Correction can happen later if necessary. Instead, these meetings are about catching your people doing something *right*. And even more fundamental, it's about getting to know them as people. One-on-ones help you find out where their pain points are, how team members are doing on their work and projects, and what they need from you for resources or removing obstacles. One-on-ones are about connection, relationship-building, *and* results. We encourage leaders to make it clear that no one's in trouble—one-on-ones are for everyone's benefit.

"First couple times I did one-on-ones with my team, the reaction was, 'Gee whiz, this is great! I've never had this experience before,'" Tim said. "I heard things like, 'Thank you for taking the time because no one is listening to me.' These are things we take for granted that don't happen, but they should be happening. I don't get people who don't spend time with their folks."

Now he schedules one-on-ones on his calendar to get to know and engage each member of his team. We're not talking about the drive-by conversations that are a part of daily work and interaction. One-on-ones are private, formally scheduled conversations with employees that occur with a consistent cadence, such as weekly, bi-weekly, or monthly. Some organizations we work with call them check-in sessions or touch bases. A standing agenda for one-on-ones can include: What's gone well since our last one-on-one? What challenges have you faced? What do you need to accomplish between now and our next one-on-one? How can I support you? The benefits of one-on-ones include self-monitoring and ownership by the employee, open communication, focus on priorities, and better relationships and support. For Tim, one-on-ones help him keep lines of communication open. *How are you doing? What help can I provide you?* He calls it Leadership 101.

Over time, Tim has goals to create more advanced leadership and implement change measures. He has hired new engineering and information technology leaders, and he wants to put in place a "scoreboard" so the team has performance metrics and knows if they're headed in the right direction. But all of that will come later. His team has to first know that this new figure in the organization cares about them. It starts, simply, with treating them as fully human.

Maybe it's no coincidence that Tim's last name is . . . Peoples. He has the skill of seeing people as people.

Action Step: Interview Your Team

One-on-one conversations, as Tim's experience shows, are one of the best ways to create alliances, forge connections, and build relationships with your team members. Over time, these conversations with each individual enable you to learn and understand what makes them tick, where their passions and strengths lie, and how they can contribute to the team according to their unique talents, perspectives, and gifts. Most important, they help you learn how you can be the best leader for each unique person on your team.

The action step on the next page provides a set of questions to ask each team member in a private conversation. You can use all of the questions, a selection of them, or add your own. Even if you already have regular one-on-ones with your team members, make this interview a "special" meeting. Frame it up for them simply as a chance for you to get to know them better and learn how they see the operations of the team.

During the conversation, remember to "let them hold the ball" and do the talking while you "peel the onion" with your questions. Also, ask follow-up questions that come to mind as you listen to understand their perspectives and points of view.

Be sure to take notes along the way as well. These interviews will provide you with a lot of good information that you can put into action.

Interview Your Team

1. What do you like most about your work?

2. What do you like least?

3. What are some things I most need to know about you?

4. What are you passionate about?

5. What are your dreams and goals, both personal and career?

6. What is working well on our team?

7. What is not working well on our team?

8. What are your suggestions for how we can make these things better?

2

LEADERSHIP IS A DIFFERENT SKILL SET

Gene and Steve started working at a small architectural firm in the late 1960s. In their twenties, they formed a friendship and partnered on projects together. Over time, they started to move up in the company hierarchy as the firm expanded from Milwaukee to Chicago to Minneapolis, Florida and beyond.

Through the decades, the company developed a strong reputation for creating innovative multifamily housing and senior living spaces. By the late 1990s, Steve and Gene found themselves at the top of a successful company with more than fifty employees. They took over, re-branded and put their own mark on the firm.

Outwardly, their company looked successful. Inside, they didn't exactly know the best way to lead their employees. They could continue to follow the management model they grew up with—making unilateral decisions as the partners of the firm—but that didn't feel like the best approach.

Like most architects, Gene said he had abundant skills to design buildings, but leading people was a completely different thing—and it wasn't what he went to school for.

Looking back today, Gene can remember only one leadership training experience in his fifty-two-year career, which he says he stumbled upon by accident. It was a series of workshops in the late 1970s about being assertive. Gene tried out the new techniques, but he didn't like having these types of discussions with his team. They were awkward and didn't come naturally to him.

"I had to really build up my courage to do that," he remembered. "When Steve and I were running this company, we didn't want to upset people. We would cover for you but not fire you."

So the training was forgotten. Instead, if someone wasn't pulling their weight, Gene figured out how to get the work done, even if that meant long nights or weekends or doing it himself.

But that approach was not sustainable. When Steve retired and with Gene approaching his seventies, he started to feel his mortality creeping in. Looking ahead five to ten years, he suddenly couldn't imagine running the company in the same fashion at that age. But he also didn't want to just be "put out to pasture," as he calls it. He wanted to be intentional about turning the company—that bears the last name initials from him and Steve—over into good hands. He needed strong leaders, not just great architects. He needed to hear from his team and from others. He needed feedback that would help.

That's when he came to us. After fifty years in the business, it was time to build an intentional leadership structure—one that empowers and puts trust in those around him, one that equips leaders with the tools to be successful and sustainable so he could turn the company over to them.

"I so much enjoy what I do," he explained of his work as an architect. "My work is a great joy, and I like doing it. But for decades, I have also felt like I'm the only guy with the skills to do this."

But he wouldn't be around forever. After his departure, change would be necessary if the company were going to move forward.

Parallel Lines

As he struggled with his transition from architect to leader and finally to preparing the next generation of leaders, Gene found himself in a situation like many people who are skilled and specialized in a technical area of expertise. We call it the parallel lines problem. Here's how it works.

Most leaders, Gene included, begin as high-performing individual contributors who do their jobs very well. Over time, these high performers find themselves taking on new projects and bigger assignments, developing their knowledge and abilities in the functions of their work, even garnering more pay and responsibility. Then a leadership position opens, and success at their job leads to a promotion. The best machinist becomes the team lead, the best nurse becomes the nurse supervisor, and the best salesperson becomes the sales manager.

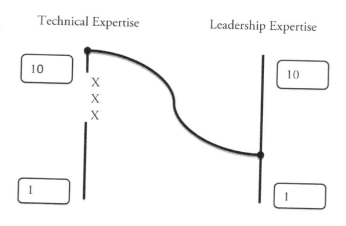

This phenomenon is true in most areas of life.

So how is this a problem? Simply put: Just because Gene was a great architect didn't automatically mean he'd be a great leader of other architects. Designing a building isn't the same as having a difficult conversation with an employee on your team. Leadership requires different ways of thinking and, ultimately, completely different skills.

> LEADERSHIP REQUIRES DIFFERENT WAYS OF THINKING AND, ULTIMATELY, COMPLETELY DIFFERENT SKILLS.

Growing Your Team

> Before you become a leader, success is all about growing yourself. After you become a leader, success is about growing others.
>
> —Jack Welch

Too often, a high performer who becomes the leader rests on the assumption that her high-performing nature will translate to effective leadership. But as we said before, leadership is about getting results through other people. And people are not like projects—humans are messy and complicated.

> "BEFORE YOU BECOME A LEADER, SUCCESS IS ALL ABOUT GROWING YOURSELF. AFTER YOU BECOME A LEADER, SUCCESS IS ABOUT GROWING OTHERS."
> —JACK WELCH

That said, high performers do instinctively lead one group of employees well—other high performers. These workers are familiar to them. They often share the same talent, ability to learn, and work ethic. With them, the leader assigns the job, and it gets done well and on time. It's easy.

But what about other members of the team?

The new leader may believe that leadership should entail nothing more than this: Set an expectation, and it gets done right the first time. These leaders, who often represent the top 10 percent of the workforce, don't think of themselves as the exception but rather as the standard for everyone's work. This leads them to struggle when leading average workers or low performers—the ones who need the most leadership to grow—to help them become better performers and to reach their potential. In these situations, leaders can become frustrated and intolerant when asked to provide more support or direction than they themselves needed. They might even lash out at the team members who don't seem to "get it."

We have also seen leaders go the other way. Their approach to underperformance by team members is to pick up the slack for them—as Gene used to do. They simply do the work themselves, or, worse yet, they assign it to a high performer on the team. While this might get the work done, it often leads to over-burdening the leader or high performer, and it doesn't do anything to help the low performer get better.

Eventually, many leaders realize that their promotion to leadership doesn't mean they have the skills needed for it. There is a new learning curve every leader must embark on. As Gene and others who become leaders discover, leadership isn't just a continuation of the same line of developing and executing on their technical skills. Leadership is a whole new space. It's a line parallel from where they started.

Reflection: Common Skills of an Effective Leader

Let's be clear about something. We're not saying your technical knowledge and skill aren't valuable when you become the leader. In fact, your technical expertise can be the very thing that helps you to coach, guide, and grow the members of your team.

What we are saying is that to be effective as leaders, we need to learn and develop additional skills and behaviors in order to get the results we desire from our teams. The good news is, leadership is learnable. It's not rocket science. Effective leadership is about taking what's common sense and turning it into common practice. For example, it's common sense that people want to be treated respectfully. Treat people respectfully. It's common sense that people need to clearly know what's expected of them to be successful at work. Set clear expectations.

On the following page, you'll find a selection of common skills, behaviors, and characteristics that enable you to engage people effectively to get desired results. Read each statement and rate yourself on how effectively you demonstrate this in your role as a leader. As you rate yourself, take stock of where your strengths lie and where you have opportunities to improve.

Rating Yourself

1 = Never, 2 = Rarely, 3 = Sometimes, 4 = Often, 5 = Always

1. I understand that everyone comes from a different place—with different skill levels, experiences, perspectives, preferences, etc.

   1 – 2 – 3 – 4 – 5

2. I treat people respectfully at all times.

   1 – 2 – 3 – 4 – 5

3. I'm humble as a leader—I know "it's not about me."

   1 – 2 – 3 – 4 – 5

4. When I'm frustrated, I manage my emotions.

   1 – 2 – 3 – 4 – 5

5. I ask questions to involve others in problem-solving and decision-making.

   1 – 2 – 3 – 4 – 5

6. I listen to people when they speak—not just to hear but to understand.

   1 – 2 – 3 – 4 – 5

7. I set clear expectations with others.

$$1 - 2 - 3 - 4 - 5$$

8. I routinely communicate priorities and performance metrics.

$$1 - 2 - 3 - 4 - 5$$

9. I coach my employees to help them learn and grow.

$$1 - 2 - 3 - 4 - 5$$

10. I provide positive, reinforcing feedback when things go well.

$$1 - 2 - 3 - 4 - 5$$

11. I provide improvement-oriented feedback when people are off track.

$$1 - 2 - 3 - 4 - 5$$

12. I recognize and reward employees for the good work they do.

$$1 - 2 - 3 - 4 - 5$$

Blind Spots

The list of skills, behaviors, and characteristics above is by no means exhaustive, but it provides a solid starting point for building awareness of how to increase leadership effectiveness. It shows how leadership expertise is different from technical expertise.

Such self-reflection is a powerful way to identify opportunities for developing as a leader. But it's just a starting point. Unfortunately, leadership gaps and deficiencies aren't always obvious to leaders. After all, they've been highly skilled at what they were originally trained to do for their careers. When they become leaders, they don't know what they don't know—they are "unconsciously incompetent," a term coined by Noel Burch in the 1970s in his work with Gordon Training International. Their training model proposes that acquiring new skills requires passing through four stages: Unconsciously unskilled, consciously unskilled, consciously skilled and finally unconsciously skilled.[7] In other words, leaders have to first see what's lacking in their skillset before they can learn, practice, and improve. Eventually, over time, their leadership skills become second nature.

But sometimes, leaders can go years ignoring or not seeing issues right in front of them. They may even wait until the end of their careers—when it's time to turn over the company (or their role) to someone else—until they deal with deep-seated leadership issues that could have been festering for years.

To make matters worse, leaders aren't always fully aware of their leadership issues because two things limit their visibility to their blind spots. The first limitation is that most employees don't willingly point out the boss's failures and foibles—at least not to the boss. Your people might talk to each other about your shortcomings as a leader, but they likely won't tell you. Second, as leaders, we don't typically **ask** for feedback on our leadership. We assume that everything is going well since no one's telling us anything different (refer to the first limitation). This reinforcing loop—not getting feedback and not asking for it—leaves us in the dark as to where our true leadership-development opportunities lie. Yet one of the best sources to learn what to improve in your leadership are the very people who are the recipients of it. The people you impact.

Without feedback, leaders can appear hypocritical. They may see the problems in colleagues or their direct reports but not notice the glaring issues in themselves that everyone else talks about behind their backs. Leaders are often more aware of how they are being treated than how they are treating the people around them. One of our clients who treats his employees terribly—we're working on this—has a sign in his office that reads "Honesty, Respect, Integrity… Always." Until we brought the hypocrisy of this sign to his attention, he had not consciously thought about his treatment of people. Like most people, leaders are keenly aware of when they are being mistreated but are blind to their mistreatment of others.

Beyond Self-Reflection

The productive alternative is for you to find a mechanism to get feedback on your leadership—feedback on what you're doing well and what you're not doing well.

Organizations use a variety of methods to help leaders get feedback about the impact of their leadership. They administer surveys, create focus groups for airing concerns, provide telephone or web-based hotlines, and hang suggestion boxes.

One of the most effective ways for leaders to get feedback is for the organization to enlist a companywide engagement survey. Engagement surveys give the organization insight into a variety of issues that are connected to employee engagement, including the impact that leaders have on their teams. The survey provides data that the organization can then use to identify and leverage its strengths and to build action plans to address the real issues in the organization.

The term employee engagement was first coined in the early 1990s and is credited to Frank Schmidt, a professor at the University of Iowa who is also a researcher for the Gallup Organization. Gallup has been at the front end of employee engagement information since the 1990s when they first started to notice a relationship between the sense of connection that employees feel to their organizations and the performance of those organizations. Over and over, research shows evidence of the costs and benefits of disengaged or engaged employees. When there is low employee engagement, organizations pay the price in absenteeism, turnover, increased accidents, and lost productivity. On the flip side, a highly engaged workforce brings greater productivity, higher customer satisfaction, and organizational profitability.

What Gallup and many other research organizations have found is that employee engagement—this emotional and psychological connection that employees feel toward their work experience—is rooted in three areas: 1) How the employee feels about their own work (the job itself, their sense of contribution, whether they have the tools and resources they need); 2) How the employee feels about the organization (its goals, mission, values, senior leadership team); and 3) How the employee feels about his or her direct leader. This third area is the key for you in developing your leadership. Research has consistently shown that you, as a leader, have the greatest single impact on employee engagement. Gallup's research argues that up to 70 percent of the variance between disengagement and engagement in your team ties back to you as the direct leader.[8]

Data from engagement surveys can start to help you spot problem areas. It's no longer about a few employees complaining if you can see the data of an entire team or department through their ratings and feelings about their work environment. Engagement surveys can benchmark your results against other similar companies in your industry to see how you compare. Ideally, these same engagement surveys should be repeated every few years to see if employee engagement goes up or down over time.

If your organization conducts an engagement survey (or another type of employee-satisfaction survey), study the results from your slice of the organization. Look for clues on what you can do in your leadership to better fill the gaps or meet the needs of your team.

An even better tool for gaining insight into your leadership skills is a 360-degree feedback assessment, also called a 360. These assessments take into account multiple levels of feedback from your direct reports, boss, colleagues, and those inside and outside the organization. A 360 gives you a full and targeted picture of your performance, key strengths, and areas for improvement. Specifically, a 360 gives you feedback on how you impact the various constituent groups you interact with and influence, especially your team of direct reports (who, as we said, often won't give you all the feedback you need). A 360 operates anonymously—you won't know what each person said (other than your boss)—but your 360 report will give you ratings and comments bundled by each constituent group. Armed with this comprehensive feedback, you will be able to identify key themes within and across the groups to create an action plan for developing skills and behaviors that will enable you to more effectively lead, influence, and communicate with other people.

If your organization offers a 360 process for you to use, use it. Contact your human resources representative right now to find out and get it going. And if your organization doesn't currently have a 360 available, before we close this chapter, we'll show you a similar process you can do on your own.

A New World

Throughout his career, no one ever trained Gene on how to become an effective leader, so he followed his instincts—for better or worse. As a result, his journey on a parallel track of technical and leadership skills was needlessly more difficult than it needed to be. But the good news is it's never too late to open your eyes.

For a half-century, Gene had been finding ways to go along to get along. But Gene knew that strategy was not an effective way to lead in the current workplace environment. He had to step up as a leader. To that end, Gene felt an urgency to get support in two areas—developing and implementing a succession plan for himself as he was looking to leave the company and building the skills of his leadership team rather than leaving them to figure things out on their own.

"One of our goals was to create a culture of leadership," he said. "In giving attention to the future of leadership in our company, one of the biggest things we learned is how to differentiate between doing and leading. We are very accomplished doers. We are not very accomplished leaders."

One eye-opening moment for Gene was accepting the fact that coaching others is what's expected from a leader. He realized that the "assertive conversations" techniques from the 1970s weren't enough. Rather, he learned through his work with us to truly have a dialogue and open conversations with his team. He learned that he needed to hear their feedback and understand what they needed from him, understand their challenges, and work with them and teach them how to solve some of their challenges.

"In the old world, a team lead or project manager would say, 'This person is not performing well, but I'll make up the difference to compensate,'" he said. "The new model is now, as leaders, we need to have a conversation with this person.

Here are my expectations, and do we have an agreement that you'll meet these expectations? And if you're not meeting these expectations, here's what we need, let's keep talking about this. It's supposed to be a two-way conversation. There has to be buy-in. For us, that's all a new world."

We worked with Gene to put in leadership principles and empower leaders around him. They created teams to develop workplace expectations, train employees, update technology, and provide personal enrichment. Gene observed and responded to generational changes that would help the company attract, retain, and develop young talent.

"No one comes to work to be a robot like I might have been when I was younger," he said. "They want full lives."

Gene opened his eyes, invited feedback from his team, noticed leadership gaps for himself and others, and took steps to build a comprehensive plan for leadership development and succession. This gave him a path to retire from his company with confidence and peace of mind. It gave him control of his legacy.

"What I have found in this whole process is the ability to let go and see that there are people who are stepping up in response," he said. "They are stepping up in the same way that I did when I was their age."

Today, he calls this a light at the end of the tunnel.

"Now I feel," he said, "like the company is in good hands."

Action Step: Get Feedback

So many things demand your time and attention, and unfortunately, the task side of your role can often prevent you from doing justice to the leadership of your people. It's time to make a conscious, intentional effort to swing the pendulum toward growing and developing your skills as a leader.

Begin the process by getting feedback on your leadership from your team. If your organization offers a 360-degree feedback tool, work with your human resources team to get a 360 going for you. If you don't have access to a 360, here is a highly effective exercise that works the same way.

We call this exercise "Keep, Stop, Start." It involves asking your direct reports to answer four simple questions (which you'll find on the next page). Just follow these steps:

1. Type the questions on the next page into a blank document.

2. Communicate to your team that you are going to ask them to participate in an exercise to give you anonymous feedback. Let them know that the purpose of the exercise is for you to get honest feedback about your leadership—what's working and what's not.

3. Send an electronic copy of the document you created to each of your direct reports. Ask them to answer the four questions, then print the document. Provide a way for them to deposit the document anonymously (e.g., have them put it in your physical mailbox or give it to someone outside the team who has agreed to collect the documents for you).

4. When all documents are in, read them. Look for the common themes that are coming up under each question. Make note of the top two or three themes for each question in an action plan for yourself.

5. Share your action plan with your team. Hold a team discussion or one-on-one discussions to get their reactions to your plan. Discuss ways they can hold you accountable.

6. Modify your plan as necessary, given their additional feedback and reactions. Share the plan with your boss. And begin working your plan!

Keep, Stop, Start

1. What do I do as a leader that you like and want me to KEEP doing?

2. What do I do as a leader that you don't like and want me to STOP doing?

3. What am I not doing as a leader that you want me to START doing?

4. What else would you like to share about my leadership and me?

3

SLOWING DOWN TO SPEED UP

Kent was shocked to see the box of cereal on Dave's desk. When he noticed it, Kent knew that this unusual decoration symbolized the breakthrough he had been seeking. He just never thought it would come from Dave, a guy who Kent described bluntly as "hard-assed." Then Dave told Kent how meaningful the box of cereal was to him and how they had to remember it whenever making decisions. Dave even started tearing up.

Why was an everyday breakfast staple making Dave so sentimental? Spoiler alert: It wasn't about the cereal.

Let's back up to 2007 when Kent joined a multi-national manufacturing company that developed parts for automobile engines. Kent had recently been promoted from his human resources manager role to become the new global leadership development manager, and he was tasked to spearhead the next phase in the burgeoning global company's growth. Previously, leadership development training was almost non-existent at the company. To take the next step, the company would have to start giving leaders the tools they needed to grow.

"Our pain point was that we had not had a training and development function within the organization for twenty years," Kent said. "We basically had a generation or two of leaders in charge who had never been trained how to do things the right way."

We first met Kent in 2012 at a small workshop held in the town that housed one of his company's plants. Our timing could not have been better since he had been researching leadership development consultants and was nearing his decision-making moment. We slipped in just in time and provided exactly what he was hoping to find. In short order, we partnered with Kent to begin facilitating training sessions and small group coaching for his leadership team.

"Having been both a trainer and leader of training organizations in the past, I knew the learning curve and the forgetting curve. So many people walk out of a training session and then rarely apply it," he said. "What stood out to me as a differentiator was small group coaching. That became my absolute favorite part. We've deployed the small group coaching concept throughout all kinds of training across the organization to make the lessons and applications stick."

Working with Kent more broadly across the organization, we implemented our comprehensive approach to developing leaders. The simple formula included our curriculum of twelve four-hour interactive workshops supported by small group coaching and a variety of content reinforcements, including real-time practice exercises, eLearning, a mobile app, and additional support tools. Over the years, our work with leaders in the company contributed to a full-company turnaround by helping to rebuild their human resources organization, establish a learning and development function, build stronger leaders, create a people development and growth mindset culture, lead change management, embed innovation into the culture, and establish talent management. It was a tall order for one of our most important clients to date.

Kent noticed that his company lacked a culture centered around people. To remedy that early on, we practiced our Box of Life training with about 120 leaders and top contributors in the company. The goal was to return to focusing on people, not just results.

"Our pendulum had swung all the way to the results side of the equation," Kent remembered. "The other side of that equation is relationships. The Living As A Leader curriculum helped us swing that pendulum from all about results back to how we get results with people."

As you'll recall, the Box of Life is an exercise that helps leaders become other-centered. They start to consider all the hidden motivations, struggles, experiences, circumstances, and other factors that go into people's actions. It helps leaders dig below the surface and see people as people. It also helps leaders to slow down to act, rather than producing knee-jerk reactions that can misread the situation and compound problems.

It was after these Box of Life sessions that Dave went out and bought several boxes of Life . . . *cereal*. He handed them out to everyone who went through our workshop, placing them on desks as a reminder. Kent recalls that Dave is someone who was born in New York and built his career in the hardscrabble plants of Detroit—not exactly someone given to sentimentality. And yet he realized it's counterproductive to rush to execution without slowing down to first understand the people who get the results. This is when Kent noticed the box of Life cereal on Dave's desk. At that point, Kent knew the lessons had taken root and would endure in the company.

"He told me how meaningful that was and that we have to remember it whenever we're making decisions—and he got teary and sentimental," Kent recalls. "Subsequently, from working with him, I learned that he was a pretty sentimental guy. He went on to build a team and become a relationship-oriented guy. You couldn't take the hard-ass out of him, but he softened it a bit."

This reminds us of another example in a different organization. After learning concepts related to the Box of Life and "people as people," a gentleman in the room shared, "I am so ashamed of myself—for how I have treated people for thirty years. I didn't know any of this stuff. No one ever taught me this stuff."

Although transformations don't happen overnight, we have seen dramatic examples. Most commonly, we focus on helping leaders see the big picture, understand people and root causes, and slow down to act. We move from short-term BAND-AIDs® to long-term solutions. Years later, the boxes of Life cereal can still be seen on shelves and desks at Kent's company as reminders of this lesson.

It's a paradox of leadership that to move forward faster, leaders need to slow down.

The Need for Less Speed

> I apologize for such a long letter. I didn't have time to write a short one.
>
> —Mark Twain

How fast are you reading this right now?

Are you skimming? Scanning? Scrolling? Moving on? Thinking about your next meeting, picking up the kids, closing a deal, or planning dinner tonight? Did you get distracted?

How about this:

S
L
O
W

D
O
W
N

Did the Message Get Through?

In the last few decades, the pace of our lives and the sheer volume of information has sped up dramatically. We are always connected to devices that send us breaking news, emails from colleagues, tracking updates on the real-time delivery of packages, texts from friends and family, and other non-stop pings, buzzes, and push notifications. In this information-saturated environment, we no longer simply read, for instance. We scan headlines and bullet points. We may soak up tidbits of data all day, but this leaves us little time to process and make sense of everything. The need for speed obscures the ability to see the big picture and create real, lasting change.

Leaders need to slow down because people need it. As leadership guru Stephen Covey has said: "Efficiency with people is ineffective. With people, fast is slow and slow is fast."[2]

This is because the human brain also hasn't completely caught up with the pace of today's digital age. You may quickly scroll through Instagram or Facebook and thumbs up and heart all the posts you like. But that's not the same as truly understanding and leading people. For that to work, there's no shortcut. When leaders try to circumvent this step, they end up creating more obstacles around them. We've seen that time and again. Like Mark Twain's reference to his long letter, we try to do more by rushing through things—but just cramming in more information ends up as rambling background noise. What gets lost when we speed up is clarity and precision. Better to take your time with a proverbial "short letter" that highlights what's really important.

One leader we worked with brought extensive experience from previous global roles—and then sought to quickly implement what he thought was best into a new organization. One employee described him as "moving very fast, almost to the point of barreling through." He did not stop to ask why things were done the way they were before trying to steamroll new practices into place. "Initially, while he said he was open to suggestions, his actions did not show it," one team member wrote in his 360 review. "We were making process changes on the fly based on how he did things at his prior company, even though the businesses were very different. Many hours and much frustration took place during this transition." The leader's reviews went on like that for quite a while, so in the interest of time, here's just one more nugget: "He has *no* appreciation for the time and effort it takes to meet his ever-changing wishes," one person wrote. "He expects everything NOW." (Emphasis original.) Ironically, in an attempt to save time and effort, this leader was making the process longer and more difficult—if not impossible.

If this person had just taken some time to slow down and listen, his employees would have warmed to him quicker. His team didn't mind improving where it was needed, but they also would have appreciated, as one employee put it, "demonstrating some respect for our success." This employee noted that "many times he is right about the need to change, but it feels like no current processes are effective when he speaks." Another person bemoaned that "it's his way or no way. That may be fine, but getting agreement, and at least listening and appreciating other opinions, would go a long way even if he plans to do it his own way—but he just brushes you off," this person added. Simply acknowledging current successes and the people behind them would have fostered a spirit of cooperation rather than resistance. As one employee noted simply, "I would like to see him make an attempt to have more informal day-to-day interaction with department members." They were craving time to bond and understand each other.

There's a proverb that often gets quoted in leadership training: If you want to go fast, go alone. If you want to go far, go together. But for many leaders, it's a natural tendency to quickly jump to coming up with solutions. They fix problems. They implement standard operating procedures. They assume they know all the answers and the best way forward. So why delay?

> IF YOU WANT TO GO FAST, GO ALONE. IF YOU WANT TO GO FAR, GO TOGETHER.

This approach may have worked in their previous roles when solutions were relatively simple and straight-forward. But as leaders, there are more moving parts. People and systems are complex. This requires a new approach that may seem counterintuitive at first. Leaders need to slow down, see the avenues to reach their goal, and build connections and buy-in before they act.

Leaders may also need to shift their timetable horizons when thinking about their people. It's easy to get caught up in a to-do list of what needs to get done by the end of the day, week, or quarter. And those tasks are important. But they also need to be balanced with an overarching goal of nurturing and developing people's talents—and that takes time. Certain crucial behaviors and activities of good leadership take patience: Listening, employee involvement that asks for team member's suggestions and ideas, coaching, having meaningful conversations, setting clear expectations, explaining the "whys" behind a change, and letting other people speak or share concerns. As Max DePree writes in *Leadership Is an Art*, "Effectiveness comes about through enabling others to reach their potential—both their personal potential and their corporate or institutional potential."[9] Leadership isn't about extracting as much as you can from others in the short term, which can lead to burnout, fatigue, or resentment. Instead, being patient and helping develop those around you leads to an even bigger reward.

Leaders also need to slow down—not just because their people need to develop, grow, and learn from others who can help and mentor them. It's also critical for leaders to take time to connect with people in deep and broad ways. Harvard psychology professor Dr. Robert Putnam defined connection—which he calls social capital—in two ways: *Bridging*, which brings together people of different backgrounds (widening your network), and *bonding* that brings together people of similar backgrounds and interests (deepening your network).[10] According to this theory, networks can either build weak ties or reinforce existing relationships. Leaders need both of these social capital building blocks before they start to implement. For this, they need to go deep and move outward. This takes time.

When leaders are new or growing in their role, they need to build a support system. This includes establishing open communication with supervisors and direct reports, but it also means building an informal network of insiders and knowledgeable colleagues who can "show you the ropes." Bridging and bonding with those around you can help you discover information that isn't in the employee job manual. Building this rapport means internal networking and treating your own people with the respect and attention you'd give someone who was giving a TED Talk or an important connection you met at a conference. It could mean joining the company kickball team, going to lunch with colleagues instead of eating at your desk, or leaving notes of gratitude on someone's desk. It can take many forms depending on your style, but the end result is deepened trust and understanding with those who work together. This may feel like it's taking time now, but it's an investment that will pay compound interest later.

As you slow down and become patient with others, it helps to think about people who were patient with you when you needed it. Who in your own network has modeled understanding? Who has listened to you when you needed it? Who has patiently asked for your feedback and involvement? Who has had meaningful conversations with you that made you feel seen? When you are struggling with slowing down, keep these examples in mind. In the next section, we'll help you find and visualize these models of your "best coach" so you can bring them to mind when they are most needed.

Reflection: Your Best Coach

> Coaching is unlocking a person's potential to maximize their own performance. It's helping them to learn rather than teaching them.
>
> —Tim Gallwey

Most if not all of us, somewhere in our past, have a "best coach." Those great coaches leave us clues as to how we can slow down to be effective as leaders.

Who was your best coach ever? Think back over your life. Hopefully, in your work, you had a boss who was a great coach for you, but your best coach might have been a sports coach from high school, a debate or forensics coach, a mentor, counselor, parent, teacher, choir director, friend, family member, or pastor.

Who was your best coach ever?

Now, with your best coach firmly in mind, consider this question: What did your best coach do (specific behaviors) when interacting and communicating with you?

On the next page, brainstorm answers to this question. Try to come up with three to five answers.

My Best Coach

What did your best coach do (specific behaviors) when interacting and communicating with you?

Best Coach Behaviors

We've done this same exercise about your "best coach" with hundreds of leaders, and every time a startling thing happens. You might have had the same experience as they do.

As we said, our best coaches give us clues as to how we sometimes need to slow down to lead most effectively. Take a look at your list on the previous page. Circle the behaviors that required your coach to slow down and take time in order to help you learn, grow, expand your capabilities, and perform at a higher level.

Here are some of the common answers we get when we ask leaders to list the behaviors of their best coaches.

- Listened

- Spent time with me

- Invested in me

- Asked for my ideas

- Let me try things and even fail

- Let me learn

- Asked me questions

How many of these kinds of answers showed up on your list? The remarkable thing is that the vast majority of answers leaders give about their best coaches involve behaviors that need time and require slowing down to let the process unfold and evolve.

A great coach knows that you aren't going to learn it all in one day, so they don't rush to see results immediately. Even Lebron James didn't dunk a shot his first day on the court. So instead, coaches focus on developing fundamentals, one step at a time. They get to know your strengths and weaknesses. Then they focus on developing and honing your skills, one by one. They do drills. Team bonding. Practices. Scrimmages. Again and again. It takes time and patience. Helping others become their best self takes longer than doing it yourself, but it's longer-lasting. Good coaching helps people move forward productively, just as your best coaches helped do for you.

Ask yourself: How well am I slowing down and taking the time to give my people what they need to grow and perform?

Remember what Stephen Covey said: "Efficiency with people is ineffective. With people, fast is slow and slow is fast."

Slowing Down for Ourselves

Many people spend more time planning their summer vacations or their holidays than thinking about who they want to be as a person or as a leader. That's why in our leadership development process, we carve out time at the beginning to provide the opportunity to do soul-searching, to consider what kind of person you want to become. Thinking about your best coach and emulating what they did is one way to build your leadership expertise. Developing as a leader is a journey, and the reality is, it takes a long time. As leaders approach this personal and professional learning curve, they'll want to think about their professional goals but also their personal motivations. To understand others, you have to first understand yourself. As ancient Greek sages instructed: *Nosce te ipsum.* Know thyself.

In our experience, we've seen that leaders can make measurable improvement early on in their development process when they start with slowing down and knowing themselves. This process takes time too. You can start by looking at data from an engagement survey or 360 assessment from your team. That's also why we do the exercises in this book for deeper understanding. If you are not yet grasping all of the characteristics of a great leader, be patient with yourself and with others and simply acknowledge that you have work ahead of you on your leadership learning journey. Great leaders are not made overnight. Developing as a leader is a lifelong pursuit. Leaders are made throughout a lifetime of steady progress, continuous improvement, and honest self-reflection. There's never a finish line for becoming a better leader. Just as if you were to take up golf or practice public speaking, there's always an aspect you can work on and refine. Developing new skills as a leader means, with practice, developing them into regular and improved habits.

For example, in one of our customer organizations, a department manager was an extremely analytical guy. He was highly competent in some areas, but he had blind spots that needed intentionality to improve over time. Part of the training process included each of the leaders gaining more self-awareness. In doing so, this manager became aware that some of the people in the company did not like him. They felt that he was not very friendly. As an analytical person, his friendlier side played second fiddle to his logical, pragmatic side. He had no idea how people felt and was certainly not being unfriendly on purpose.

Once he realized the issue, it took time and deliberate action to change perceptions others had of him. He had to take a step back. The change didn't happen overnight. As part of his intentional leadership approach, he identified a few key behaviors he could practice. He made a point of coming out of his office twice a day to chat with some of his staff members. "I might ask them something about their weekend or give them some positive feedback about something they were working on. I'd even try to smile more often," explained the manager. Just a few minutes each day, over time, made a huge impact. These simple gestures, rooted in practicing new behaviors, are examples of leading by design, or intentional leadership. And the approach worked—people noticed the difference. And they were willing to take the journey with him.

As a great Chinese proverb tells us: "The best time to plant a tree was twenty years ago. The second best time is now." So whether you started on your leadership journey twenty years ago or you're just getting started, make it your intention to keep it moving forward.

> WHETHER YOU STARTED ON YOUR LEADERSHIP JOURNEY TWENTY YEARS AGO OR YOU'RE JUST GETTING STARTED, MAKE IT YOUR INTENTION TO KEEP IT MOVING FORWARD.

Forward with Integrity

Remember the leader who rubbed everyone the wrong way by his impatience and wanting everything now, now, *now*?

Things actually got better over time.

One employee wrote in the leader's next 360 review: "The first six to twelve months I had a very difficult time—his way was 'best' without understanding why we did things the way we did. But I also have to admit that he has gotten better over time. Perhaps it's just my relationship with him, but I've seen significant improvement. Maybe we've gotten more used to each other. There are still issues, but not like it used to be. He made some impressions early that were not favorable, but I have had the opportunity to work with him enough to change my initial impression."

That's the thing about time: It may not heal all wounds, but it can at least make a bad situation better. If the leader had been more patient earlier, he could have saved a lot of conflict and ill will during the first year. Think about how much more progress he could have made by simply being more patient and moving slower. We realize that the business world is a results-oriented culture. There is a lot of pressure to perform. Leaders sometimes feel like they don't have the "luxury" to move at what feels like slower progress, even if they are hurting their cause in the long run with excessive speed.

The antidote to moving forward haphazardly is to intentionally design how to behave for the best results. This is why we frequently reiterate the need to get feedback from your team so you can use that data to start intentionally designing your growth as a leader. Most leaders have good intentions. No one wakes up in the morning and thinks, *I wonder whose day I can ruin?* They want their team members to be effective. They want to be able to lead well. They want to help people grow and contribute. They want to be seen as good leaders. They want to be liked by their people. We believe, deep down, that the vast majority of leaders—including the person reading this—are good people with good values. They want to do good in the world. To accomplish this, it's necessary to lead by design.

We have a model we call Integrity Circles. It helps us to understand the impact of our behavior as leaders.

Integrity Circles

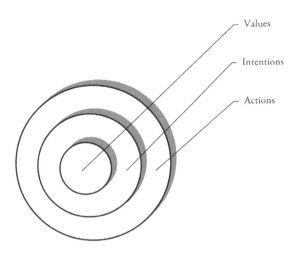

Imagine you are made up of three concentric circles: The innermost circle represents your values, the middle circle your intentions, and the outermost circle represents your behaviors and actions. Integrity, which means holding true to your values in what you say and do, is present in you as a leader when there is an alignment of all three circles—Values + Intentions + Behaviors = Integrity. This takes constant work to keep the circles in alignment.

VALUES + INTENTIONS + BEHAVIORS = INTEGRITY.

Let's take Kent as an example of a leader who works to keep his circles in alignment. Kent considers himself as someone with a high empathy rating who knows how to have sensitive and productive conversations with his teammates. He values empathy and intends to display that in his interactions. However, there are times he finds himself getting frustrated with others who aren't on the same page as him, which can cause his behavior to outwardly show impatience. That's when he has to remind himself to go back to his inner circle, which contains his value of empathy. He reminds himself that everyone has a different Box of Life. He thinks of the box of Life . . . cereal. This helps him come back to building a bridge with the other person, rather than creating discord and disconnect. His empathy value guides his intentions and actions. Ultimately, this approach is more productive.

"I always have to remind myself not to have a NER—Negative Emotional Reaction," Kent said. "There's often a difference between what someone says or does and your interpretation. You always have to be very careful about that."

Ultimately, Kent sees leadership as a higher calling—more than just a title or a means to an end.

"Leadership," he said, "is an expression of the true self." For him, leadership reveals true character over time.

Action Step: Model Your Good Values

We have talked about the importance of leaders seeing people as people, taking time to understand them, how to energize them positively, and how to lead them best. We have discussed the distinction between leading and doing and how leaders need to take a step back, trust others to do the work, and use their own technical expertise to guide and grow their teams. These are all ways to slow down to speed up.

We also believe it's important for leaders to ensure that their words and non-verbal actions match up. Are they saying they have an open-door policy, but their closed-off demeanor and harried actions communicate the opposite message? Do they claim to care about people but become noticeably frustrated when personal situations impact the ability to get work done? Your people will notice the disconnect. That's why leaders need to model their values and intentions.

When we work with leaders, we share a set of guiding principles of leadership that we ask them to keep in mind and to begin modeling in their actions. In fact, these principles are woven into the fabric of what we do and the process we use. These principles speak to the character of the leader. All three take patience and time to develop into habits. They are also three areas where it's easy to stumble into a misalignment of word and action if we're not careful.

Be Kind—Many leaders think that kindness will diminish their ability to be effective. However, kindness does not mean being a pushover or a doormat. Successful leaders understand being kind, pleasant, or affable to their employees will encourage and motivate them to be far more productive. It is also one of the least expensive, least time consuming, and simplest ways to make a positive impact as a leader.

Show Humility—Leaders who are humble do not believe they are the smartest or most talented people in the room. They do not live as if it's all about them or that they're perfect. Instead, they recognize, as a leader, they have both strengths and weaknesses. In fact, they not only have weaknesses but can also acknowledge mistakes and even own up to them. True humility also means putting others in the limelight rather than yourself, which is far more appealing than arrogance.

Show Tolerance—Remaining calm when things are not going well, remaining patient when people make mistakes, accepting that people are different, and having grace under pressure are hallmarks of a strong leader. Tolerance means accepting other people for who they are, including their strengths and weaknesses. People respond better when leaders are calm and don't become emotionally intolerant.

On the next page, consider these three principles as potential areas to model good values as a leader. Answer the questions related to how you can practice kindness, humility, and tolerance, then for the next three days, practice the actions you select for yourself in all of your interactions at work and home.

These principles will require you to slow down. You will need to think about them and remain mindful in order to practice them, but we're confident that they will help you be even more effective with others.

Model Your Good Values

1. What is one way you can practice kindness in your interactions and communication with others over the next three days?

2. What is one way you can practice humility in your interactions and communication over the next three days?

3. What is one way you can practice tolerance in your interactions and communication over the next three days?

4

GREAT EXPECTATIONS

B rian and the leadership team at ERDMAN met offsite for two days. At stake was the future of the company. It was exactly fifty years after Marshall Erdman, an immigrant from Lithuania who pioneered a new approach to healthcare design and construction, had founded the business in 1951. When Erdman died in 1995, his obituary ran in the *New York Times* and noted his collaborations with famous architect Frank Lloyd Wright.

While growing the business, Erdman was known for doing things his way, from start to finish. Erdman hired architects, engineers, construction managers, and other support staff to work together in one firm to deliver medical offices. He believed in an "everything-in-house approach"—now called integrated project delivery—and built his own factory for prefabricated building components. Even the finishing touches of the art reflected the personal style and sensibilities of the founder. As an ardent art collector, Erdman commissioned his staff to provide art to office buildings—but clients had to abide by the choices. After they lived with it for a year, if they didn't like it, they could get their money back. By the 1990s, the company had completed over 2,500 buildings and was the leading provider of small healthcare clinics in the country. It was a testament to Erdman's success that influenced the American building industry.

Not surprisingly, the shadow of the influential founder hung over the company as they entered a new millennium. Even as they looked to the future, they straddled the past. The company, now located in its own beautiful four-story building in Madison, Wisconsin, is on a street named for the firm—1 Erdman Place. A mural and quote from Frank Lloyd Wright greets visitors when they walk into the company's expansive lobby. The design of the building was a nod to the founder and an intentional step into the future.

Yet after the legendary founder had passed, the company found itself without a rudder. The leadership team fell victim to infighting and passive-aggressiveness. In one instance, an associate took Brian out to lunch and told him to pick a side. An engagement survey found that trust in the executive team was 42 percent. (For comparison, 2020 data indicates 96 percent trust in the senior leadership team.)

"The company was starting to fall apart, frankly," Brian remembered. "There were a lot of things that were broken."

The instance of culture collapsing after a founding leader leaves a company is so common that it has a name—Founder's Syndrome or *Founderitis*. A charismatic and passionate leader can hold together a company by sheer strength of will. But this can also cover up deeper underlying problems that rise to the surface when that leader is no longer in charge. Without defining clear expectations, chaos and uncertainty can ensue.

Changing the culture may be the holy grail of leadership because it's so encompassing and difficult.

Culture is all the norms, beliefs, actions, and ways of doing things—both formally and informally—that guide a group of people. Culture must be assembled and reassembled with care and clear expectations. Words, actions, and inactions all shape the culture over time, piece by piece and day by day. If leaders don't set out to deliberately shape the culture, the culture will take shape for them. The longer a company has been around and the bigger it becomes, the harder it is to make major shifts in the values, beliefs, and behaviors of the organization. It's like trying to turn an ocean liner—it takes time and energy.

That's why Brian and his team entered an offsite room together to decide how to lead the company through its next phase. To define new expectations. The culture was not what it once was, they acknowledged. The culture was exactly what it had been, passive and waiting for direction. It didn't fit the new vision of the company; it hadn't evolved. The poor engagement surveys reflected that. So they started to discuss what behaviors they wanted to see at the company—and what needed to be eliminated. With that simple meeting, they started to discuss how to change the culture of a company more than a half-century old.

It started during those few days. The complete turnaround took years and is still in progress. There are no shortcuts in the process. It starts with clearly defining expectations. In this chapter, we will discuss the important and fundamental role of setting expectations in leadership, employee development, and overall results. If the expectations are great, performance will follow.

Defining Expectations

Expectations are the very basis of all performance. We like to call them the "rules of the game." Expectations, clearly defined, repeated, and reinforced, lead to the behaviors within the team that shape a high-performing team culture. Whether you are building a culture throughout a company or developing the culture of your team, the same principles apply. The basis of expectations for culture is the same regardless of context; a leader can influence culture in their sphere of influence, no matter how big or small. We find that most leaders we work with—whether that leader is a front-line supervisor or a VP who oversees a large department of multiple teams—most leaders really want to become effective at developing a high-performing team culture. That starts with clear expectations.

> EXPECTATIONS ARE THE VERY BASIS OF ALL PERFORMANCE.

Data and research back up the importance of expectations. Over the course of thirty years of research into employee engagement, Gallup has methodically prioritized the most fundamental aspect of work into this one statement: "I know what is expected of me at work." Employees who can positively answer that question tend to come from productive teams, while those who can't tend to come from low-performing teams. Gallup has been able to further attach metrics to the outcomes of clear expectations: "knowing what's expected" alone often correlates with productivity gains of 5 percent to 10 percent, thousands more happy customers, and 10 percent to 20 percent fewer on-the-job accidents.[11]

Zenger Folkman's research brings an added benefit. Their research shows a strong correlation between being seen as a leader who sets clear expectations and being seen as a leader who is motivating and inspiring. They write, "There is obviously something about being clear that is closely linked with people feeling motivated and inspired."[12] So, if you want to be a motivating and inspiring leader, start working on setting clear expectations.

Ensuring that expectations are clear up front helps your team know what successful performance looks like. Ultimately, you cannot adequately build a high-performing team if you're not first clear on what you expect from your employees. And they can't perform at a high level if they're not clear on what you expect. Think of expectation-setting as a form of visioning—creating a vision for the desired behaviors and standards of your team. Clearly defined expectations save time, money, and energy because they focus everyone on what's really important for the team and organization.

As leaders, we not only need to define expectations, but we also need to continually clarify and revisit them. Do expectations shift and change from time to time? Of course, they do. Are people ever unclear about what's expected of them? Yes, they are. A key to great leadership is keeping expectations top of mind for people, as well as adjusting and re-defining them as needs change.

If you don't adequately plan for, clearly define, and continually clarify the specific expectations for employee performance, you increase the likelihood that there will be unmet expectations and frustrations down the road. Yet, let's be clear: *setting expectations is more than just defining performance and then telling people what to do.* How we discuss and talk about expectations, how we collaborate with employees when creating them, and how we listen to their thoughts and feedback and questions about those expectations—that's what creates alignment, agreement, buy-in, and commitment. Involving employees in the process of defining and clarifying expectations increases the likelihood they'll embrace and agree to the expectations and be successful at meeting them. A collaborative approach unleashes their energy, enthusiasm, and effort.

Remember these four ways to ensure maximum buy-in whenever you're defining and clarifying expectations:

Involve Employees—Do everything you can to involve others in the process of defining, clarifying, and agreeing to expectations. As Jack Stack said in his book *The Great Game of Business,* "People will support what they help to create."

Be Prepared—Be clear for yourself on what's required for employees in terms of expectations. If you're not clear, how can they be clear? And if they're not clear, they can't buy in and perform.

Be Flexible—As you involve employees in setting expectations, be open to their ideas and suggestions. Let them shape the direction with you. Your flexibility will further foster their buy-in.

Build Trust—Always be mindful of building trust with your team. What does trust have to do with their buy-in? People will follow you only to the level that they trust you.

Reflection: What Are Your Expectations?

Expectations for your team come from a variety of places. A job description, for example, is a set of expectations for a particular role. Your organization's values often drive expectations for how we want people to behave and operate as they do their work. Goals are also a category of expectations that identify specific performance objectives or targets, which often reach beyond the day-to-day activities and responsibilities of a person's role or job function.

When we first start to help leaders think about and clarify their key expectations for their teams, we share with them a simple framework. We find this framework helps leaders to brainstorm the different types of expectations that are important for high performance on their teams. The framework also helps them sort and organize their different expectations.

This framework includes three categories that signify three high-level areas of workplace performance: 1) Conduct (behavior), 2) Attendance (time), and 3) Performance (standards). We believe that every expectation we have as leaders falls into one of these three categories. They are listed below with examples:

1. **Conduct: Workplace behavior, including personal and interpersonal interactions.**
   ✓ "Members of our team do not talk about others behind their back."
   ✓ "Do not use profanity under pressure."
   ✓ "Treat everyone with respect."

2. **Attendance: Time-related expectations for being at work (attendance) and being on time for work-related functions (punctuality).**
   ✓ "Arrive no later than 8:00 a.m."
   ✓ "Put in at least eight hours a day."
   ✓ "Arrive at meetings on time."

3. **Performance: Expectations related to standards—completion of work; adherence to procedures; efficiencies; and quantity, quality, and timeliness of work.**
   ✓ "Meet all deadlines or talk to the person you're accountable to if a deadline needs to be changed."
   ✓ "Continually look for and suggest ways to improve our processes."
   ✓ "Do what you say you'll do—follow through."
   ✓ "Dedicate time each week to work on your long-term goals."

Depending on how your team operates, you may find that some of these categories are more relevant than others. For example, in today's workplace, many leaders and organizations are more flexible regarding time than in decades past; the members of your team may not have specific starting times each day. Yet you probably have time-related expectations of your team that still fall into this category, such as being on time for meetings or communicating to the team when they'll be out of the office.

Using this framework, begin the process of brainstorming your key expectations for members of your team in each of the categories. Start with any category you like and move about freely. This is simply a brainstorm to get the ideas of your key expectations "out on the table." Later, in the action step for this chapter, we'll show you a way to refine the set of expectations, involve your team in the process, and begin using the newly minted expectations with your team.

What Are Your Expectations?

- Conduct (behavior)

- Attendance (time)

- Performance (standards)

Moving Beyond Expectations

As we said, clear expectations "set the bar" for what good performance looks like. They enable your team to know where to focus their efforts, how to perform, and what to commit to in order to be successful.

Clear expectations also help you lead. They help you set in place clear direction and standards with each member of your team and ensure that you both are in alignment and agreement about performance in its most crucial facets. With that foundation in place, we like to tell leaders to memorize this mantra: "As a leader, I don't manage people. I manage the agreements I have with people."

Managing to the agreements you have with your team around expectations is what helps you lead. It becomes the way that you manage performance—not because you're doing the work for your people but because you're now set up to know what to pay attention to. Expectations help you know what to focus on, what to track, and what to monitor. They give you a leadership roadmap for knowing when to praise, acknowledge, and recognize people for doing good work (because they're hitting the agreed-to expectations); and they give you the heads-up and red flags that indicate when it's time to coach and re-direct because someone's falling short.

Once expectations are set and agreed to, the next step for you is to monitor the expectations. The term "monitoring" may conjure an image of Big Brother looking over employees' shoulders, making sure they're not checking Facebook all day and ensuring they are always productive. That's not what we mean. Monitoring is NOT micro-managing. Instead, monitoring is the process of being intentional and mindful about tracking expectations, having strategies for gauging performance, and paying attention to progress over time. Because, if you don't pay attention, how can you and your employees know whether they're staying the course or need to course correct?

There are four key methods for monitoring performance:

1. **Observation** is simply observing people in real-time as they do their work or as you interact with them. It could be watching them as they conduct a process, or it could be noticing how they conduct themselves in meetings. The list goes on and on, and what you observe will be based on the work they do and what you expect from their performance.

2. **Collection of data and feedback.** This could include reporting or metrics you track related to performance. Or it could include feedback you solicit from other people or teams that your employees interact with or work with.

3. **Check-in discussions.** These are discussions you have with employees for them to report to you or update you on some aspect of performance: a follow-up item, progress on a project, a milestone on a goal, whether they have completed a task, etc. These may be informal touchpoints or formal meetings and discussions, such as regularly scheduled one-on-ones or weekly team meetings.

4. **Self-monitoring** by employees. These are strategies you use to encourage employees to track their own work, such as performance reports, checklists, or weekly updates on progress.

Monitoring is an ongoing process that works best when you build it into your schedule and document performance along the way. For consistent monitoring to work effectively, there are two important ideas we encourage you to keep in mind:

First, intentionally and mindfully make time—schedule it. Put it on your calendar as an action as important as any meeting or project. Second, document ongoing progress and performance toward expectations. Keeping notes and documenting your monitoring throughout the year is a crucial responsibility as a leader. It also makes recognizing good performance or coaching for improvement a lot easier because you'll have facts and details to back them up.

In the next chapter, we'll talk more about coaching. For now, know that for coaching to be effective, leaders need to create the foundation with clear expectations and consistent, quality monitoring. In fact, all three of these pieces—setting expectations, monitoring performance, and coaching—are interdependent and interrelated. As examples: If you aren't clear about expectations for yourself and your team, how can you know what to look for and monitor? If you don't monitor effectively, how can you know how and when to coach and give feedback? And if you don't coach, how can your team clearly know whether they're on track in terms of expectations for performance?

Putting the Pieces Together

In those few days holed up in a room, Brian and his team at ERDMAN put together two simple lists. On one side were the behaviors they wanted to see—including being constructive, talking to a person, not about them, and doing the right thing for the client. On the other side were the behaviors they wanted to eliminate—including passive-aggressiveness.

It all starts with individual changes. If you can't change the culture overnight, you can at least begin to influence the climate. Over time, the pieces will fall into place.

Kim Albrecht, who has been a facilitator and coach at Living As A Leader for more than twenty years, works with her clients to focus on making measurable progress bit by bit.

"Culture is usually something that's been established over a long period of time," Kim said. "But we can influence climate." Climate is defined as the conditions that characterize a period or group. "So the more direct influence you have, the more likely the area in which you're leading can be changed. We have more influence over climate without a doubt. Within a year's time, leaders can make an impact in the people they lead."

Effective leaders can begin to affect cultural shifts by modeling the way. A lot of leaders say they "lead by example," which is a starting point. It also means modeling what we're asking for from others. Our people do watch us when we're leaders. Modeling is about integrity, walking the talk, putting forth from ourselves the things we also expect from others.

One caveat: Leading by example is an important, fundamental aspect of good leadership, but it is also insufficient. It's a crucial starting point but can't be the only thing. There is more to good leadership—we must also demonstrate and engage. Others will sometimes miss what leaders are modeling, so leaders must also define expectations, reinforce the good, redirect the not-so-good, and continue to do the work of shifting the culture. Culture-building is a daily task.

We worked with ERDMAN's leadership team to set and reinforce expectations. We met with senior leaders, managers, and high-potential employees. Their expectations became part of the words they used, the behaviors they exhibited, and even the visuals—like "Be All In"—hanging up around the building. As a result, some people left the company when they did not meet these expectations. Those who remained embraced the common mission. The culture arose out of a shared sense of expectations, given different roles. It took time, but it was deliberate. It brought together the disparate parts of the company into a more holistic unit.

"Under one roof in-house, we have designers, architects, engineers, construction managers, estimators, human resources staff, marketing, and consulting," Brian said. "You have to have an environment where they can work together and all solve issues together. It's not just about the technical competency; you have to know how to work with people from very diverse backgrounds. When that works well, it's awesome. Our clients feel that, the team feels that."

Over time, we helped them build a leadership program. They retooled an employee recognition program to reinforce those who exemplify the company's leadership and values. The ERDMAN Excellence Award rewards leadership and behavior instead of simply years of service or technical proficiency. Six people were nominated by their peers when it was re-rolled out, and a year later, it grew to twenty-nine peer nominations, all high-quality submissions. Award winners receive a monetary award, a vacation, and a package where they can customize their trip with personal time off. They are recognized at a company-wide event. The nominator talks about the finalist, and it gets the whole company involved.

Being clear on what the company is—and isn't—has helped them attract new talent. People want to work where they can see themselves fitting in, and they can only envision themselves if the company has set clear expectations of what its culture entails. With the labor market in its industry at its tightest in fifty years, they were still able to hire twenty new top professionals last year. New recruits came to Wisconsin from Chicago, Michigan, Rhode Island, Texas, and beyond.

"We're shocked that we're able to do that—our No. 1 challenge is recruitment," Brian said. "ERDMAN is specifically looking for candidates who can exhibit and practice our leadership and our values. We made it more programmatic, and that momentum is going up. That story starts to get out about our brand and our culture. They're choosing us because it's a special place to be."

It also helps them differentiate when they are presenting to potential clients.

"The feedback we get from our clients is it feels different to work with you," Brian said. "We now incorporate talking about our culture into our presentations to clients and internally. The people you are going to meet and deal with are well and good-intentioned, collaborative people. It sounds subtle, but when you go through a big capital project, it's about the journey together."

The business results followed and increased along with the changes to culture. Soon, after making the initial changes in the early 2000s, the company tripled the size of their pipeline and almost quadrupled earnings. Today, they are again on that trajectory. The company has reshaped its values and expectations in the decades after it emerged from its founder's shadow. The former Marshall Erdman and Associates is now called ERDMAN, and they have adopted an identity that both upholds their traditions and looks forward. They build health care and senior living facilities that serve communities throughout the country. Their hundreds of employees do work they are proud of that matters. And they expect to do more.

Action Step: Create an Expectations One-Pager

An expectations one-pager is a document that clearly lays out the most critical expectations you have for members of your team. Think of the one-pager as a list of ground rules or operating principles. It's like the constitution for your team.

You can organize your one-pager using our three categories from before—conduct, attendance, and performance—or you can organize it using another framework that already exists in your organization, such as your company's list of values. An important consideration as you create your one-pager is to keep it focused. Your team members aren't going to be able to remember twenty-seven expectations. Your job is to focus the one-pager on the critical few. A maximum number of five to seven expectations is a good target for your one-pager. If you divide it into three categories, for instance, you'll have no more than two to three expectations for each category.

Here's how to build an expectations one-pager:

1. Revisit your earlier brainstorm of possible expectations you might suggest for your team. On the next page, refine the list to include only the most critical few expectations in each category.

2. Type up a draft of your one-pager and share it with your team. Discuss it. Hear their feedback, questions, and ideas for improving the clarity of the expectations.

3. Modify, adjust, and revise the one-pager based on team feedback.

4. Roll out and publish the one-pager.

Once you publish your expectations, that's only the beginning. Be sure to develop ways to keep them alive and top of mind for yourself and everyone on the team. Develop systems for yourself to track and monitor your key expectations. Revisit the one-pager regularly and revise it as needed. Treat it as a "living document."

Developing and discussing an expectations one-pager with your team is also an excellent time for you to get more clarity about what they expect from you as their leader. Ask that question during your discussions and incorporate those additional expectations as a separate list within the document.

My Expectations One-Pager

5

COACH, DON'T CONFRONT

Cathy didn't want to be a CEO—at least not at first. Prior to joining a non-profit health insurance start-up, she was an executive director for a small health co-op serving farmers and agri-businesses. She had no direct reports in that role. Yet she found herself becoming CEO after just two years into working at her new company, having previously served as chief operating officer.

"I had imposter syndrome," Cathy said. "The way I came up into the CEO position, I regularly questioned myself, 'Should I be here?'"

In the early days of the start-up, she found she could let little things slide because the company was simply focusing on survival. She justified avoiding conflict or being direct when people were missing on expectations because there was no time to put in all types of protocols and enforce rules. Different styles were simply allowed and accepted as part of start-up culture.

As the company grew, however, it became increasingly apparent that Cathy needed to be direct and actively coach her team to improve performance in certain areas and take the business to the next level. It was the last thing she wanted to do. But she also had a high willingness to do better. That's when she brought in Rick, one of our coaches at Living As A Leader. She knew she needed help to allow herself to be the leader she needed to become.

"There was a lot to unpack there," she said. "I wanted to say I had a problem. I had to self-reflect, *'What is my role?'*"

Cathy thoroughly discussed with Rick what was really holding her back from having direct and clear conversations with people when performance was slipping. During the conversation, Rick helped Cathy "peel the onion," one layer at a time, until she got to the core of the issue. She realized she feared being regarded as a mean boss. She didn't want to be seen as ruling with an iron fist.

"Rick helped me go pretty deep," Cathy said. "I grew up with an authoritarian father. Authority was very negative to me, and it was scary. So I know, because of that, I wasn't properly exercising my authority as CEO. Some of the issues that were developing were a result of me not leading with authority."

For a long while, Cathy told herself that she wasn't avoiding conflict. To prove it, she said, she had made the hard decision to fire people who needed removal from the company. But was that really addressing conflict? Peeling the onion to look deeper, she said, revealed examples of not resolving under-lying issues as they came up. The firings may have relieved symptoms, but she wasn't fully addressing the root causes, so problems would return.

"I had check-ins with employees, and I said I'd bring it up when they weren't hitting deadlines," she remembers. And then she would forget or put off further check-ins. "I convinced myself, subconsciously, that it wasn't that bad. I told myself they only missed some deadlines. I justified it."

Cathy needed to change her perception of what it means to be a leader. Taking charge is not negative when used to set expectations, provide clear direction, and give direct feedback, especially when it's done in a respectful and candid way. In fact, employees crave structure and feedback when used consistently and with intentions to help both the company and the employee. Leaders don't need to have confrontations. They need to have conversations.

Working with Rick, Cathy learned communication and coaching techniques to exercise her authority in a way that focused on the behavior, not the people. This transformed Cathy's whole idea of how and why good leaders don't confront—they coach.

"Authority isn't about firing people," she said. "It's about coaching people and holding them accountable for behavior change. Make your expectations really clear."

Leading, as Cathy learned, isn't simply about being strict or demanding. Instead, it's about embracing the leadership role to help and coach others to serve the greater needs of the organization. As Cathy grew into her role, she recognized that true confidence would come from trusting and coaching when it is needed. Today, she is comfortable using her leadership role and her coaching skills to hold her team accountable.

Balancing Accountability and Inspiration

More than 500 years ago, the philosopher and scholar Niccolò Machiavelli wrote *The Prince*. Today, the term Machiavellian is still associated with the idea that leaders need to be sneaky, manipulative, or iron-fisted in order to maintain control. The phrase "it's better to be feared than loved" is commonly cited from his work to justify authoritarian behavior from leaders.

Even though Machiavelli did not exactly advocate for compassionate and understanding leadership, his most famous saying is almost always taken out of context. The full quote is as follows: "It would be best to be both loved and feared. But since the two rarely come together, anyone compelled to choose will find greater security in being feared than in being loved." Machiavelli may have acknowledged the difficulty of balancing fear and love, but he never said, as many people now falsely attribute to him, that it has to be one or the other. That's a false choice. Leaders need both.

Today, we work with leaders on the same dilemma that Machiavelli noticed half a millennium ago. We just use slightly more modern workplace terminology. We don't want anyone to fear their leaders, but they should feel accountable. Leaders also don't need to be loved like a cult of personality, but inspiring and energizing their team should be the goal. We call this balancing accountability and inspiration:

> LEADERS ALSO DON'T NEED TO BE LOVED LIKE A CULT OF PERSONALITY, BUT INSPIRING AND ENERGIZING THEIR TEAM SHOULD BE THE GOAL.

Accountability involves things like managing employee performance on an ongoing basis, including defining expectations, monitoring performance, giving feedback, and setting goals.

Inspiration involves listening to people, involving them in decision-making, encouraging them, praising their progress, and facilitating their interaction with others.

Leaders are innately wired either to lean toward the accountability of getting work done or toward inspiring and motivating people to do their work. In other words, there are leaders who focus only on results, results, results (but often struggle to inspire and engage) . . . and leaders who show care and concern for people (but do not always effectively hold them accountable for desired results). As we referenced in the introduction to this book, accountability and inspiration are like two oars of a leadership rowboat. We need them both, and we need to be good at them both. Overemphasize just one, and you end up rowing in circles. We help leaders balance the scale by learning how to coach using both sides of the equation. And yes, it may feel uncomfortable at first to go against your natural tendencies.

In our workshop, "The Seven Most Common Mistakes Leaders Make," one of the major mistakes we talk about is the imbalance between accountability and inspiration. It is the balance between the two that drives both results and employee fulfillment. Because, as we mentioned, most leaders will lean more toward either accountability or inspiration; that tendency will have a real impact in terms of leadership effectiveness.

We get it: It can sound like more fun to be inspirational than hold your team accountable. That's why many leaders, when faced with difficult situations, choose to avoid them. It's the flight aspect of fight or flight. They don't know what to say or what to do, so they do nothing. Other leaders react by instinct and attack rather than having a conversation. Obviously, this is the fight instinct kicking in.

When leaders timidly or aggressively exercise their authority, it confuses their team. In one situation, our team worked with a woman, let's call her Sue, who was a very talented engineer and quite capable as an engineering manager. She was good at troubleshooting, making quick decisions, and moving things forward. Her leadership, however, was not inspirational. Part of her disadvantage was that her boss was extremely uncomfortable discussing the areas where she needed to improve and didn't hold her accountable. By not talking with Sue candidly, he was not helping her. She needed a boss who was able to help her see her blind spots to improve. When they talked, his demeanor was of someone who had to deliver bad news but didn't know how to bring it up. Her style, in contrast, was very direct and quite defensive. She immediately blamed others. He viewed the conversation as a punishment and kept apologizing. Essentially, it sounded like, "You are so good at what you do; I'm just so sorry to have to bring this up and make an issue of it." His exhale was audible as he walked out the door, relieved, as the conversation had mercifully ended.

Typically, leaders themselves tend to fall back on their human instincts and defense mechanisms. Leaders who tend to fight basically tell others to knock it off, shape up, get your act together, etc. Leaders who tend to take flight may try to have less interaction and let their responses show up in more subtle ways, such as being written in an annual review months after the fact or cloaked within a reminder message to the entire team when it's really a message for just one person. In the above scenario, the boss, being much less assertive, might not have done anything—which would not have resolved the situation. But it would have, at some point, come to a head in some manner.

When talking privately with Sue, we made sure she understood that she was not supposed to have this all figured out, and her defensive response represented natural human instincts. She felt relieved to learn that she was not a bad person and was, in fact, in good company among many leaders with whom we've all worked. With an understanding that we would be focusing on where she would be going and not obsessing on her mistakes, she opened up to working together. She confirmed that she wanted to do well, and she was open to receiving help.

This is a key to using authority effectively: Leaders need to make it clear that holding their team accountable doesn't mean others are bad employees or bad people. Instead, it's about unlocking their true potential to deliver on expectations.

Reflection: Your Leadership "Home Base"

As you think about your own leadership, identify whether you lean more toward accountability or more toward inspiration. "It depends" is a common answer when we pose this question, but as we said, each of us tends to lean toward one or the other. It's our starting point. Our home base. Your answer will reflect your most common tendency.

Consider your preference for accountability or inspiration: How is it expressed in what you say or do? What is the risk of leaning more toward your preference? What does the other style offer that you need to provide as a leader?

When we do this exercise in groups, we invite everyone who feels they lean more toward accountability to go stand at the right side of the room and those who lean more toward inspiration to stand at the left side of the room. Typically, it's about a fifty-fifty split. One style isn't better than the other—we need both. It's helpful to know your default position, so you can work to develop the appropriate counterpart of leadership.

For this exercise, the next page is split in two. On the left side, write down all the things you do to hold your team accountable. Then on the right side, write down all the things you do to inspire your team.

When you are done, look at the page. Are both columns roughly equal, or is there an obvious imbalance? If there is an imbalance, you know you have work to do to bolster the style that's falling short. Brainstorm some additional things you could do to enhance this style and bring the two into balance.

Balancing Accountability and Inspiration

Ways I Hold My Team Accountable	Ways I Inspire My Team

Coaching for Improvement

As stated earlier, coaching is a style of communication. Our tendency toward accountability or inspiration shapes how and whether we have coaching conversations when people fall short of expectations. We all have a natural tendency to fall back on what we feel most comfortable doing, even if that isn't always the most effective given the situation.

COACHING IS A STYLE OF COMMUNICATION.

We also know, when we need to talk about missed expectations, the conversations *themselves* aren't always comfortable. Two key factors make coaching for improvement difficult. First, many expectations that get missed relate to conduct and behavior (which can often feel tricky to deal with). It's one thing to be able to point to a clock and let someone know they're late; it's another thing to talk to someone about how they mistreat people or storm off when they're angry. Second, as leaders, we have our own very common and human pitfalls to deal with, including our tendencies to make assumptions, get emotional, blame others, and get self-centered. Combine these tendencies with our overall lack of skill and experience with how to have tough conversations effectively, and you can understand the difficulty.

Getting comfortable with uncomfortable conversations is a fact of good leadership, and it takes patience and practice. If you're like most people, no one taught you how to have a "tough talk" in a clear, direct, constructive, and respectful way. No one taught you how to carefully prepare for such conversations, so you could set the tone as non-confrontational and then approach people in a way that acknowledges them, values their concerns, does not cast blame, and allows you to stay calm. People are predictable: they get defensive, and they will self-protect if they feel they are being attacked or "called to the carpet." If you set the stage in a non-accusatory, non-personal manner, it changes the dynamic.

> GETTING COMFORTABLE
> WITH UNCOMFORTABLE
> CONVERSATIONS IS A FACT
> OF GOOD LEADERSHIP, AND
> IT TAKES PATIENCE AND
> PRACTICE.

Our Coaching for Improvement process provides a six-step framework and structure you can use to prepare and deliver coaching conversations when people are straying off track. It's a learnable and flexible method that works well in any situation, regardless of the expectation that's not being met. You can apply it in any of the three areas of expectation we discussed in the last chapter, whether your employee is coming in late (time and attendance), missing deadlines (performance standards), or struggling to work well with others (conduct). Best of all, the process works because it is intentionally designed to help you have a conversation that simultaneously enhances accountability to expectations while also inspiring and engaging the employee. It's the very method Cathy learned from Rick.

The premise behind the Coaching for Improvement process is this: When you prepare a conversation proactively and communicate "by design"—with specific attention to the words you choose and approach you use—you get a much better result. So often, as we've said, we avoid these conversations. We allow situations to escalate and eventually handle them with frustration, intolerance, and poor choice of words. Then we wonder why we don't get the result we need.

Below, you'll see our Coaching for Improvement process. It begins with an invitation to have a conversation followed by a six-step framework for the conversation itself. We'll explore each step, share its rationale, and suggest what it might sound like in your communication and dialogue with employees.

Invitation
Step 1: Welcome
Step 2: Set the Stage
Step 3: State the Facts
Step 4: Ask a Key Question
Step 5: Ask and Listen
Step 6: Gain Agreement

Invitation. The process begins with an invitation to meet at a time that is convenient for both of you. A key to having a tough, effective conversation is to treat it as a *collaboration* rather than a confrontation. Your goal is to team up with the employee to solve a problem. By inviting your employee to have a conversation with you and doing so at a time that works for them, you're sending a signal that it's a collaborative event. An invitation like this is a huge departure from the boss who simply storms up to an employee and shouts, "In my office. Now!"

Here's what the invitation might sound like:

Joe, I'd like to meet with you for about twenty minutes sometime today.

What time is best for you?

While we ask in the invitation if we can meet "sometime today" (or whatever your timeframe), some employees, particularly because of anxiety over what they might have "done wrong," may ask to meet right now. Don't take your authority lightly. Asking your employees to have a conversation with you can easily trigger them to think, *Am I in trouble?* So before you invite an employee to a conversation, make sure you've prepared the additional steps below to be ready for that event. Getting the timing right is important here, too, because you don't want to pick a busy time for the invitation when stress is already heightened, but you also don't want to put off issues and let them linger and fester.

Step 1: Welcome. At the start of a conversation, welcome your employee to the conversation. Thank them for being willing to meet with you, connect with them on a human level, and verify that the time is still good. This shows respect, shows that the other person is as important as you are, and that their time is valuable. This approach creates a personal atmosphere that supports collaboration, minimizes defensiveness, and sets a positive tone that builds rapport.

> Thanks for meeting with me.
> How is your afternoon going? (Listen.)
> Is this still a good time?

As we've said, you'll find it helpful when coaching for improvement to treat the conversation as a collaboration. Intentionally opening the conversation as we describe helps you do that. And if your employee says, "You know, an issue just came up with a customer. Can we do this tomorrow morning?"—then reschedule for tomorrow morning.

Step 2: Set the Stage. Once you and your employee settle in, briefly explain your intentions for the conversation and express your desire to hear the other person's thoughts. This step lets your employee know that there's an important issue to address (it's a serious conversation) while also letting them know they'll get a chance to talk (remember collaboration).

> Joe, I wanted to meet because I have a concern about something. I'll briefly share my concern, and then I'd like to hear your thoughts.
> How does that sound?

The key words here are "concern" and "hear your thoughts." Concern is a very different and neutral word from *mad* or *frustrated*, yet it still gets the employee's attention. And it's important for employees to know that they'll have an opportunity to share their perspectives. Notice, too, that you haven't yet shared the particular concern. Your goal here is simply to set the stage that you want to have a dialogue about an important issue and solve it together. It helps the employee get ready to listen and collaborate with you.

As well, notice the question at the end of the statement: "How does that sound?" This simple question continues the thread of collaboration, and the answer to it gives you an indication as to whether your employee is ready to go.

Step 3: State the Facts. Now we get into the specifics of the conversation. Here, you name the issue clearly and factually by explaining the *actual behavior* you observed and the *desired behavior* going forward.

Of all the steps, this can be one of the trickiest. And it's one of the most important to get right. This is not a time to speak from your assumptions, stories, or emotional reactions. This is a time simply to focus on the facts. Facts are your observations, thoughts, perspectives, insights, and background items you know. Facts are derived from the neutral, sensory data you observe in someone's behavior. Most often, we gather facts through what we see and hear.

Below are examples of what this step might sound like in three different situations. Remember, this step includes two elements: first, a statement of *actual behavior*, which describes the observable facts and is signaled by the words, "I noticed"; second, a statement of *desired behavior*, which describes the expectation going forward and is signaled by the words, "The expectation is …"

Joe, *I noticed* that the last two days you got into work after 8:00.

The expectation is that you're at your workstation, ready to go, every day by eight.

Mary, *I noticed* over the past week that you've missed two project deadlines.

The expectation, as we've discussed before, is that you complete projects on time or proactively let me know if there are problems, so we can strategize together.

Jess, this morning, while I was in our management meeting in the conference room, *I noticed* through the window that you were talking with Scott from sales. And through the door, which was closed, I heard you say to Scott, "You're ridiculous!" Then I saw you walk away.

I wanted to talk about this because *the expectation is* that you communicate effectively with other employees and, if you're finding that challenging, to seek my help.

By stating the facts as succinctly and neutrally as possible, you place the emphasis on the situation and behaviors, not the person. This helps the other person feel less defensive and more willing to collaborate and dialogue with you.

For you as the leader, facts foster accountability by helping you be direct about the situation at hand. A focus on facts also helps to keep you from monologuing or droning on and on so you can get to the conversation. Coupling your facts with your statement of expectation for desired behavior, you are forming a mini gap analysis between the current state and desired future state. This approach enables you and your employee to clearly know the issue to be solved so you can start problem-solving together.

Quick tip: As you prepare to coach for improvement in any situation, if you are struggling to get past your assumptions and frustrations to identify the facts, here's the best trick we know: Ask yourself, "What did I see, and what did I hear?" Those sensory observations are your facts.

Step 4: Ask a Key Question. This is where you hand the conversation over to the other person and begin the dialogue. One question here is all you need. The question should be broad and open-ended. It's intended to invite a response that ushers in a dialogue.

Here are examples of a key question you could ask in each of the scenarios above.

To Joe: What can you tell me about this?

To Mary: What are your thoughts?

To Jess: What happened this morning?

In our view, this is the step where coaching really begins. As we like to say, "Coaching starts with questions." This is the point where you turn the conversation over. Ask your question, then stop talking.

We'd also point out that the best question to use at this point is <u>not</u> a question that points at solving the problem—at least not yet. For example, hold off on asking, "What are you going to do to fix this?" It's a fine question, just not at this point (as you'll see in a moment). This is the time to hear your employee's story and explore the issue together.

Remember what Stephen Covey said: "Seek first to understand, then to be understood."

Step 5: Ask and Listen. We call this "The Conversation Box." This step is the heart of the conversation, where the two of you will spend most of your time discussing the issue and possible actions for solving it. Every step to this point is designed to bring us here. The previous four steps, if well-planned and crafted by you, will only take a few minutes. This step is the meat and potatoes of your coaching conversation.

Now, you get to hear your employee's input and learn more about the situation from their perspective. You get to understand your employee's point of view and engage them in the process of exploring their own performance. You're letting them "hold the ball."

As they share their thoughts and perspectives, you listen and ask further questions to "peel the onion," questions like:

Tell me more about . . .
What's an example of . . .
What else do I need to know?
Help me understand . . .

Through these questions, your first goal in this step is to fully understand the situation, to gain deeper understanding rather than providing your own perspectives and opinions. You've already shared those. Share additional perspectives and opinions only as necessary. Spend time asking questions and listening.

As you and your employee unpack the situation, clarify and confirm what you're hearing and understanding. Then ask questions that start moving toward action. Build a bridge to the final step by discussing possible solutions.

How would you like to solve this?
What are your thoughts on the next steps?
What do you need from me to help?

Throughout Step 5, let the other person take the lead, let them hold the ball. You peel the onion. By doing so, you engage and involve the employee in discussing, modifying, and improving their own performance, and you build their buy-in and commitment.

Step 6: Gain Agreement. Finally, in gaining agreement, the two of you work to clarify and understand what will be done to correct the actual behavior to meet the expectation, along with anything else necessary to resolve the issue, including your responsibilities and commitments as a leader to help the situation.

> It sounds like you will . . .
> and I will . . .
> Am I correct about that?

Next, collaborate on timelines, deadlines, and any agreements that need to be made regarding follow-up action or future discussions.

> What timelines and follow-up can we establish?

Finally, summarize the agreements. Repeat and clarify the commitments to action and next steps to make sure you're both on the same page moving forward. You should again work to reinforce the other person's new direction and thought process to ensure that you both are in full alignment.

> To make sure we're clear, the expectation is that you will . . . by (timeline/deadline).
> I also will . . . by (timeline/deadline).
> Is there anything I missed?

At the end of the conversation, thank the person for their time and willingness to discuss the issue with you. Provide additional words of support, such as, "I'm confident that you'll be successful moving forward." It can also be very helpful for you to write down or document the final agreements or have your employee email them to you after the conversation.

Lastly, we find that many of the leaders we work with, when they begin using this process, short shrift or even skip Step 6. We encourage you not to do that. Clarifying and confirming what we're agreeing to and how it will play out is crucially important so that miscommunication, misalignment, and further disappointment don't result. As William Whyte reportedly quipped, "The single biggest problem in communication is the illusion that it has occurred."

> AS WILLIAM WHYTE REPORTEDLY QUIPPED, "THE SINGLE BIGGEST PROBLEM IN COMMUNICATION IS THE ILLUSION THAT IT HAS OCCURRED."

Final thoughts about the process: You may have already realized that Steps 3 and 4 in the process are where your planning comes about before the conversation. What you'll communicate there is always unique to each situation. The invitation and Steps 1 and 2 are essentially the same each time. And Steps 5 and 6 arise organically from the conversation itself.

While you can't plan for what will happen in Steps 5 and 6—after all, you don't know what your employee will say— you certainly can prepare the types of questions you might ask when you get to Step 5. The majority of your preparation will be crafting your statement of fact in Step 3.

To help you use and employ this process, at the end of this chapter, we'll provide you with a comprehensive planning worksheet. The workshop where we teach this process is called "Communicate by Design," and we call it that for a very simple reason: We want to emphasize the importance of being planful and intentional about your coaching conversations that are focused on improvement. These conversations can often be difficult. They can feel contentious, as if we're in a conflict. They can also be difficult for the other person because you're asking them to change something about their performance or behavior.

Armed with the planning tool and this process, we encourage you to practice with it. Practice doesn't make perfect. Practice makes permanent. By formally preparing for coaching for improvement conversations and following and practicing this method, over time, you cement the framework into your own awareness and ability. Eventually, through practice, you will become so good at the process that you often won't need to plan in advance. You'll be able to step right into coaching conversations and automatically and successfully follow the process.

> PRACTICE DOESN'T MAKE PERFECT. PRACTICE MAKES PERMANENT.

When you communicate by design—in a purposeful, planful, and intentional way using this method—you empower yourself to have more effective coaching conversations and increase the likelihood of a desirable outcome. We hear from leaders we work with all the time that this process works for them! And as they continue to use it, they get better at it, figure out how to adapt it to new situations, and become more confident in having conversations, not confrontations.

Simply put, coaching people for improvement is about clarifying and reestablishing expectations, listening to and engaging employees in the process, and forging agreements with them around those expectations. As we said in the previous chapter, expectations "set the bar" for what good performance looks like. As a leader and coach, expectations comprise the full complement of things you want and need from your people for them to be successful in their roles. Remember, effective leaders engage other people to deliver desired results. Expectations serve as the foundation to make that happen.

Addressing the Behavior

After getting to the core of the issue with the help of Rick, Cathy realized that what made her so uncomfortable about coaching others to improve performance was that it seemed like punishment. She didn't want to become the authoritative parent, doling out punishments to misbehaving children. She didn't want to breed resentment at work in the same way she felt resentment as a child.

A transformation happened for Cathy when she started addressing a behavior like missing deadlines rather than simply punishing or avoiding the person missing the deadline. Having the conversation using our coaching method helped uncover root causes Cathy wasn't aware of: People were stretched beyond their available capacity to accomplish their work. Deadlines were either too strict or too wishy-washy. Workers had to choose between hitting one deadline or missing another. Cathy learned that the system itself—and not just the people within it—needed fixing. And Cathy had the authority to make things right. Taking this newfound information one step further, she formed a task force to come up with solutions and action items.

"Since we did that," Cathy said, "we have not missed a deadline."

Now Cathy is comfortable with coaching. She makes expectations clear and follows through with accountability. If a member of her team loses their temper, for example, she simply calmly addresses the behavior: "Losing your temper is not acceptable behavior at this organization. My expectation is you will manage your emotions." She then follows up with additional coaching, support tools, action steps, and even training to help her team meet these clear standards. She uses her authority not to force people to change but rather to enable them and empower them to make commitments to new behavior, follow through, and meet expectations. She's a coach.

Cathy has learned that authority doesn't mean showing anger or punishing others. It's just the opposite—it's about calmly stating and upholding expectations. When she realized this, Cathy says this has changed her as a person, not just as a CEO.

"The impact of this work has impacted me professionally and personally," she said. "I think that when I started with Rick, I was kind of judgmental. I made judgments about situations as positive or negative all the time. I would describe myself now as calm and centered. We might make a misstep at work, but we'll find our way through it. Don't call these things problems. They are situations."

She also brought this attitude home, and it helps her with her thirteen-year-old son as the family learns to navigate his teenage years. He missed some assignments at school, so Cathy responded by having him sign a coaching agreement—just like they do at her work. She doesn't get angry; she just sets, discusses, and enforces expectations. Focus on the behavior that needs correcting, not the person.

Cathy isn't the only one bringing work home in a positive way. She found that the authority she avoided, due to her own upbringing, has now helped her the most after she embraced it. It gives her the most satisfaction when she sees these techniques help others live their own lives better outside of work.

"I believe you should work somewhere you have joy, but it has to make you a better person," she said. "It has to be about more than just the work you do. If I can help someone to be a better person, then I feel like I have done something great with my life."

Action Step: Have the Conversation

Think of a situation with a team member where an expectation is not being met, or there is an opportunity to re-set or clarify an expectation. You'll find this exercise in your Resource Guide and as a stand-alone planning worksheet, both available at www.livingasaleader.com/book.

Using the planner, along with the step-by-step description above, prepare your "script" for your conversation with your team member. After you complete your script, role-play the conversation with your own leader or a trusted colleague to practice and refine your approach. Then have the conversation!

Coaching for Improvement Pre-Planner

What is the general issue or topic for this conversation?

For State the Facts:

What are the factual
observations?
I've noticed . . . (actual
behavior)
-
-
-

What is the expectation?
The expectation is . . .
(desired behavior)

-
-
-

What is the **impact** of the actual behavior (for Ask and Listen)?

What is the possible **consequence** if there's no change in behavior (for Ask and Listen)?

What is your **positive intent** for the other person through this conversation (for Ask and Listen)?

Coaching for *Improvement* Planner	INVITATION I'd like to meet with you for about ___ minutes sometime today. What time is best for you?
1. WELCOME	Sample Language:
• Show gratitude	*Thanks for meeting with me.*
• Connect	*How are you doing? (Listen.)*
• Verify time	*Is this still a good time?*
2. SET THE STAGE	Sample Language:
• State "concern"	*I have a concern about something.*
• Outline the discussion	*I'll briefly share my concern, and then I'd like to hear your thoughts.*
• Get reaction	*How does that sound?*
3. STATE THE FACTS	Sample Language:
• Briefly share *factual observations* (actual behavior)	*I've noticed . . .*
• State *the expectation* (desired behavior)	*The expectation is . . .*
4. ASK A KEY QUESTION	Sample Question:
• Hand over "the ball"	*What can you tell me about this?*

5. ASK & LISTEN	"T h e C o n v e r s a t i o n B o x"
• "Peel the onion" by asking questions to understand	*Tell me more about . . .* *What's an example of . . . ?* *What else?* *Help me understand . . .*
• Add your perspectives only as needed	
• Share the *impact*, *consequence*, and/or your *positive intent* as needed	
• Ask about options for moving forward	*How would you like to solve this?* *What are your thoughts about next steps?* *What do you need from me?*
• Add your thoughts about options	
6. GAIN AGREEMENT	Sample Language:
• Verify new or modified actions/goals/behaviors	*It sounds like you will/I will . . .* *Am I correct about that?*
• Collaborate on time-lines and follow-up	*What timelines and follow-up can we establish?*
• Summarize agreement	*To make sure we're clear, the expectation is that you will . . .* *I also will . . .* *Is there anything I missed?*

6

SOLVING PROBLEMS

Dimé was a young and rising star performer. She started working at a large manufacturing company at age twenty-three. A year out of college, she was already managing a full department and overseeing a team of about forty. She seemed poised to rocket up the leadership ladder and grow in the company.

Though the company offered many opportunities to rise through the ranks, her career seemed to stall. She felt stuck after working there for a decade. She was stymied by multiple issues. One particularly challenging one was a direct report, Jessica, who intimidated her and resisted feedback.

"We had personality clashes," Dimé said. "I don't know where it broke down. Somewhere she lost respect for me."

Then Dimé applied for another leadership role and didn't get it. She no longer saw herself as a young star performer whose path to leadership seemed inevitable. She had taken some one-off leadership classes but didn't have a consistent approach in learning how to be a leader. She felt adrift and didn't know what to do next.

Meanwhile, at another company, Dave started a new role as a supervisor. With a military background, he was learning how to relate to his employees without simply giving orders and waiting for them to take action. Dave was stationed in San Diego for five years as a Navy second class petty officer, where he worked on Morse code, navigation, and other duties. When someone was told to do something, they did it. There was no other option.

"In the military, your personality doesn't matter," he said. "As a supervisor, I'm going to say it to you the way I'd say it to anyone else."

But that didn't work in the work world. He was walking into a role where he led others who had more experience than him, and he perceived that this might cause friction and resentment if he didn't address it. He realized that personalities did matter if he wanted to find the best way to motivate people, not just bark orders. To build credibility and succeed in his new role, he had to adapt and learn how to be a different kind of leader.

Tammy was a listener, not a talker. The idea of having to run a meeting stressed her out. She thought, as a leader, she had to know all the answers if anyone asked her a question. She had technical knowledge, but she doubted her ability to deal with difficult conversations. Her style with problems was avoidance, which she knew wasn't working.

"If you allow the behavior to keep going, it will keep going," she said. "I was wired to just ignore it."

Frank felt overwhelmed as a new leader with direct reports who didn't get along. It was personality clashes between generations, a millennial and a boomer, with Frank caught in the middle. Throughout his whole career, Frank was a drafter who worked on his computer alone. If there was a conflict, he preferred to stay quiet and not say anything. He didn't think he had the knowledge or confidence to step up and act. Now, he had no choice but to take action.

A key part of the essence of leadership is the art and science of problem-solving. And those are skills needed by everyone, not just CEOs and founders. We all run into obstacles in our daily lives, at work, and in our families. The four leaders in the stories above had problems they needed to solve regarding how they approach their own leadership, yet as leaders, their problems could have just as easily involved operational or procedural issues, customer complaints, or defective parts on a manufacturing line. To solve any problem at work and in life—whether it's building the confidence to deal with difficult situations or finding the right continuous-improvement training for your team—we need skills and models to solve problems. In this chapter, we will discuss how to recognize, evaluate, and then confidently move forward with resolving problems as a leader—and how to better support problem-solving within your team.

> TO SOLVE ANY PROBLEM AT WORK AND IN LIFE— WHETHER IT'S BUILDING THE CONFIDENCE TO DEAL WITH DIFFICULT SITUATIONS OR FINDING THE RIGHT CONTINUOUS-IMPROVEMENT TRAINING FOR YOUR TEAM—WE NEED SKILLS AND MODELS TO SOLVE PROBLEMS.

Leaders Solve Problems

A leader who was put in charge at his company had plenty of experience and training to take over. But he wasn't quite sure where to start on his first day. So he sought out the advice of a mentor. What should I do to begin? "It's simple," the mentor replied. "Go into your office, close the door, and start making decisions." Of course, the issues that land on a leader's desk are not usually an easy call. They get to higher and higher levels because they are difficult decisions. The more senior the leader, the more complex and multi-faceted the problems they have to face.

That's why, put simply, leaders need to be experts at the problem-solving process. Of all the topics we work on with leaders, teaching them how to be better at problem-solving and helping their people do the same is one of the toughest. We believe a big reason for this is that the human process of problem-solving is complex. And no two problems are completely alike. Psychologists who study the human process of problem-solving tell us that decision-making is always part of the problem-solving process. If we don't decide on what to do or what to try, we can't solve it. Some even argue that every decision we make in life is intended to solve some sort of problem—if you need to decide on something, there's a problem you're solving, if even a small one.

For example, if you're deciding at the start of your work-week which projects and tasks to work on that week, you're solving a problem—your current state is a lack of clarity about what to get done that week, and your desired state is a sense of focus for the week. In this way, throughout our lives, we are solving problems and making decisions constantly. As philosopher Karl Popper said, "All life is problem-solving."[13] The same is true in business and organizations.

No matter where you work, days are filled with problems related to operations, customers, supply, coordination, and countless other issues. As a leader, you are the main problem-solver for your team. Your problem-solving ability is often a big part of what got you promoted to leadership in the first place. Demonstrating problem-solving ability is a valued skill in organizations. It gets noticed and promoted because it's part of how we're able to bring technical expertise to life and solve business problems.

As humans, we all want to avoid problems as much as possible and have smooth sailing. But from another perspective, if your job was that hassle-free, a robot could probably replace you. Your human ability to work through complexities is what provides value and why you are promoted to leadership.

To take the next step, leaders need to help their teams be better at solving problems themselves. While leaders will have to be the ultimate decision-makers on some issues, hoarding that power will create bottlenecks, slow-downs in the process, and create burnout for leaders that shoulder too much of the load. We hear this complaint from leaders all the time: They want team members to be more self-sufficient on matters of problem-solving, rather than coming to their supervisors too often to help. Leaders need to help their teams become more solutions-oriented. We especially hear that organizations of all types today are very focused on continuous improvement, yet leaders complain about their people not being innovation-minded or being willing to look for ways to solve problems and make things better.

Part of helping people be their best is helping them develop good judgment to move past obstacles. When we're talking about problem-solving and decision-making, we're really talking about people's judgment—their ability to judge a situation or problem, come up with effective and creative solutions, and decide confidently on the best path forward. And that means, in part, that we as leaders need to create the climate, learning opportunities, and experience people need to develop in this area—while also minimizing risk to the team and organization. As Dr. Kerr L. White famously quipped, "Good judgment comes from experience; experience comes from bad judgment." Leaders need to become comfortable with these learning opportunities, knowing that empowering others may result in short-term uncertainty but long-term growth.

From Naming to Deciding

Let's dig a little deeper and look at some of the business problems that you and your team are facing right now. The Oxford English Dictionary defines a problem as a matter or situation regarded as unwelcome or harmful and needing to be dealt with and overcome. It can also be a thing that is difficult to achieve. We view problems as both of these things. Some examples of problems in an organization could include:

Third shift not producing enough parts

Need to design a website within two weeks

Customer complaint calls are rising

Accounting software keeps breaking

A vendor is going out of business and needs to be replaced

Need a more advanced level of capability

What do you notice about all of these problem statements? They're all short. One of the fundamental but often overlooked aspects of good problem-solving and decision-making is to begin by clearly stating, as succinctly as possible, the problem we're trying to solve. This is a crucial piece for helping others become better problem-solvers. If you perceive a problem but can't clearly define it, the problem will persist as generalized stress and anxiety, without any clear outlet. Before you can make decisions, you need to understand the problem. Once the problem is clearly stated and defined, you can start to take steps to solve the underlying issues. Even when the problem seems to be obvious, it helps to engage in taking time to name the issue to ensure that your decisions are sound and not based on faulty assumptions or mistaking the real issue.

Another way to think of a problem is this: A problem is the gap between the current state and the ideal or desired state. In other words, it's a problem simply because it doesn't currently match what it is we want. If your team's new software program keeps breaking, that's a problem because you want the software to work consistently, seamlessly, and without interruption. A decision is a commitment to a course of action to close the gap. If we want to solve the problem of the software breaking, we'll need to decide what to do, who to involve, how to adapt to the software, or how to work around it until it's fixed, and so on. These are all

> A PROBLEM IS THE GAP BETWEEN THE CURRENT STATE AND THE IDEAL OR DESIRED STATE.

decisions that we believe will allow us to close the gap.

Now we can move onto the decision-making steps. Up to now, we've talked a lot about problems and problem-solving, yet this chapter is about problem-solving *and* decision-making.

When thinking about problem-solving and decision-making, keep in mind: Problems and decisions are interrelated. Problems require commitments to action if those problems are to be solved. Clarity of both the "current state" and "desired state" is crucial for effective problem-solving.

You'll notice the word is "decisions"—with an *s*. To solve any given problem usually means deciding on multiple actions that will help us close the gap between current and desired states. Often, as we go through the process of solving a problem and taking actions along the way, we learn new information, discover other options, and make new decisions about things we'll need to do to solve a problem. This is important because, too often, we see leaders and other professionals look for that one magic bullet to solve a problem. And usually, that's not realistic.

Now think about how you normally make decisions on a day-to-day basis. Chances are, for most things, you "wing it" based on your past experience and what you think might work the best. Another term for this is intuition and experience. In fact, intuition and experience play important roles in effective problem-solving and decision-making. By intuition, we mean things like hunches and gut decisions. The biggest risk, though, is that we sometimes consider our hunches as facts, or we rely too heavily on quick gut decisions. While hunches might be spot on at times, it's important to test them and analyze them. In his book *Thinking, Fast and Slow*, Noble prize-winning economist Daniel Kahneman explains how we all make quick calculations in a rapid-pace and complex world. In some ways, gut decisions are a defense mechanism that saves time and resources. While our instincts can serve us well, fast decisions can also carry the most risk if we make a wrong move.[14]

As for experience, this relates to something called the knowledge domain. The more experience we have in an area or domain of knowledge—whether sales, or business accounting, or even home plumbing—the better we are at solving those specific problems. But vast experience in a specific domain can also bring with it a risk. Our experience locks us into solutions that have worked in the past but might not work this time. In other instances, our experience may come up empty in response to a new problem. This is what Tammy feared when it came to problem-solving, thinking she may not have all the answers. In fact, it's impossible to be completely prepared by experience.

And that brings us to our next concept: Even when the problem in front of you has an obvious solution, it helps to engage in *active* problem-solving to ensure that your decisions are sound and not based on assumptions or biases. Many times, our decisions based on experience are correct, but other times we might be smart to take a step back, learn more about what's going on, and brainstorm and explore new options. Plus, when problems involve others, engaging them in intentional problem-solving rather than just giving them the answer will help them learn more deeply and become better problem-solvers in the future.

So if you can't fully trust your intuition or experience, how do you make decisions? How can you best involve others? We'll explore that model next.

Reflection: Your Problem-Solving Teaching Style

Part of our mission in this chapter is to deconstruct, demystify, and bring greater clarity to problem-solving and decision-making—so we can help our teams do it better.

Below, we've compiled thirteen elements that can help you, as a leader, increase your effectiveness at building strong problem-solvers and decision-makers around you. Some of these elements you are probably already using. We think you'll discover some new strategies as well. Read through the list of ways to create the conditions and opportunities in which you can help others grow, learn, and develop as problem-solvers and decision-makers.

To foster a favorable workplace climate:

1. Leaders PATIENTLY ACCEPT that employees have different levels of skill in problem-solving and decision-making—for some, these skills must be cultivated and developed over time.

2. Leaders INVOLVE their employees in the process of problem-solving and decision-making, rather than doing it all for them.

3. Leaders EMPOWER people to solve problems and make decisions—they give employees explicit permission to do so, even setting the expectation that problem-solving and decision-making are parts of their work.

4. Leaders CREATE A SAFE ENVIRONMENT, where employees can experiment, take risks, and try new ideas and approaches.

To develop others' capabilities:

5. Leaders help employees BUILD EXPERIENCE by delegating and assigning new tasks and projects that expand employee skills and responsibilities.

6. Leaders ASK QUESTIONS of employees to stimulate their abilities to think analytically and creatively.

7. Leaders encourage employees to ENGAGE OTHER PEOPLE (beyond the leader) in their problem-solving and decision-making efforts.

8. Leaders OFFER TRAINING that builds employees' skills and knowledge, as well as specific training that strengthens critical and creative thinking.

To model effective problem-solving and decision-making:

9. Leaders MANAGE THEIR OWN BIASES and assumptions in the face of problems to avoid limiting the problem-solving process.

10. Leaders CLARIFY THE CURRENT STATE (the real problem) and THE DESIRED STATE (end goal, outcome, objective) upfront.

11. Leaders clearly DEFINE THE CRITERIA for solving problems and making decisions—they detail relevant constraints, must-haves, resources, time requirements, strategic requirements, organizational values, etc.

12. Leaders intentionally COMMUNICATE DECISION-MAKING RIGHTS so in each situation, employees understand how decisions will be made and who has the authority to decide.

13. Leaders FOLLOW UP on problems and decisions to support the process, foster persistence, ensure accountability, and encourage continuous learning.

Considering these thirteen elements, complete the two self-reflection questions on the next page. Your self-assessment, through the lens of these thirteen elements, gives you a starting point for how you can strengthen your team and others as problem-solvers and decision-makers. You'll also find that many of these thirteen elements are baked into the problem-solving process we'll dive into in the next section.

Your Problem-Solving Teaching Style

1. List two elements that are strengths for you. Describe why they're strengths:

2. List two elements that are opportunities for you. Describe why they're opportunities:

Drinking the CIDER

We believe that one of the best tools for helping yourself and others become better problem-solvers and decision-makers is to have a process for problem-solving. Such a process breaks problem-solving into steps that others can learn and follow. It also gives us a framework to know where people struggle and, therefore, where we can help them. The problem-solving process we'll share is called CIDER.

CIDER is an acronym that represents the five steps in our problem-solving process. If you were to do an Internet search of problem-solving processes, you'd find dozens of them. Some are four steps, seven steps, eleven steps. Yet, regardless of how many steps we break the process into, all versions follow the same overarching flow of key concepts. The five steps are:

Clarify the problem.

Focus on understanding the real problem completely, rather than focusing simply on symptoms. Define the desired state.

Identify ideas and possibilities.

Delay the selection of solutions by actively seeking other ideas, possibilities, and alternatives to consider (brainstorming).

Decide on actions.

Weigh the ideas that have been generated, along with their implications and potential impact on others. Decide on what to try.

Execute the plan.

Put the decisions and actions into play.

Review and evaluate outcomes

Gauge the results of the actions taken and their effectiveness at bringing about the desired state. Return to earlier steps as necessary.

Next, we'll dig into each step in more detail.

Clarify the Problem

One of the keys to good problem-solving is to spend adequate time and energy in this first step. The more we invest in clarifying the problem and the desired outcome, the better our results generally are. People who struggle with problem-solving and decision-making can quickly become much better by simply learning how to clarify the problem effectively. One reason: Effectively clarifying the problem makes the next step much easier, sometimes even effortless—it's the brainstorming step.

Identify Ideas and Possibilities

Two things about this step: We often shortchange our brainstorming and discovery of new ideas, possibilities, and alternatives. Let's make our exploration active and intentional. Second, this is a creative-thinking step, where the only goal is to **generate ideas**. It's not a time to criticize or analyze—only to brainstorm a variety of possible actions and solutions. Critical thinking about those ideas happens next.

Decide on Actions

In this step, we narrow down our options. This step reminds us to think critically about the pros and cons of our ideas and their possible consequences and impact before pulling the trigger. And remember: Solving a problem (especially a complex one) often entails multiple decisions and actions. There is no "magic bullet."

Execute

Take action! Here's where we try things. Problem-solving and decision-making are often about running experiments—placing bets on, and then testing, solutions that you think might solve the problem.

Review and Evaluate Outcomes

While we have presented the five elements of CIDER as **sequential steps in a process**, the process of problem-solving **isn't usually linear**. For example, as you execute your actions, you may learn something new that provides a fresh idea for solving the problem. Or, as you review and evaluate outcomes, that step might lead you to decide on a new action you can take. Problem-solving is an iterative, holistic process—not always linear or logical.

One final thought: To some of you, this problem-solving process may seem plain and even obvious—likely that's because, as a good problem-solver yourself, you already follow these steps, intuitively and automatically. But remember: We also need to help others be better at problem-solving and decision-making. Having a process like this helps you to frame it for others, to teach and guide them on how to do it, so you can help them build their own capacity, insight, and mental models for how to tackle problems.

From Problem to Solution

Dimé first reflected on and stated her problem: *She stopped advancing and felt stuck.* Why was this happening to her? She had so much experience, so why didn't that help her move up? So she clarified the problem (the C in CIDER) and identified ideas and possibilities (the I in CIDER) by talking with others and getting their perspectives. She learned it was actually her history and experience that was holding her back instead of moving her forward.

"When I got started there, I was young. I made mistakes," she said. "And sometimes those mistakes followed me. There was obviously something that was holding me back, and it was my history."

Past history like a subpar performance review, a project that went over budget, or difficulties with colleagues can feel like a burden to carry around. Dimé had kept trying to push through, falling back on her instincts and intuition. In dealing with problems with the direct report we had mentioned earlier, Jessica, Dimé kept meeting and telling her what to do—because that's all she knew to do. And that approach only made Jessica's attitude worse. She was openly going on her phone and muttering things under her breath in meetings. In meetings with Jessica, Dimé found herself talking 90 percent of the time—and nothing changed.

"It had been a lot of me trying to coach her, and I was not seeing results," she said. "She was very resistant to feedback every time I gave her feedback. It was a lot of the 'oks' and no action."

Dimé knew she had to do something to get unstuck. This situation with Jessica was added evidence that something was holding her back, so she started identifying ideas and possibilities for trying something new (the I in CIDER). She knew she wanted some leadership training, but she didn't know what that would look like. She considered the one-off workshops she had taken in the past. But she knew those lessons hadn't stayed with her.

"I think the only way you can grow is to learn," she said. "And I wasn't learning anymore."

She talked with her supervisors in her company, and she learned that others in her company had worked with Living As A Leader. So she *DECIDED* to take action (the D in CIDER) and join our program. She enrolled in our leadership training and coaching in 2017. She was the first person in her branch of the company to participate in our training.

As the training started to equip her with new skills, Dimé started EXECUTING her new knowledge (the E in CIDER) to help with problems, like a difficult conversation with Jessica. She went into a meeting with our six-step coaching for improvement process. It was still hard, but Dimé stuck to the steps. In the last step, she had Jessica restate the expectations. Dimé affirmed and gained agreement. And it worked.

"Without the framework, I would have gone off topic or shut down," she said. "When we got into this meeting, and I went through each step, Jessica realized I was meaning business. After this meeting, there was action. Her behavior immediately shifted in the team meetings."

When this worked, Dimé didn't stop with just keeping these techniques for herself. Now she continues to REVIEW and use the leadership principles today with her new team (the R in CIDER). It worked because she was soon promoted. Her team has more than doubled to nearly 100 people.

"I refer to all the concepts still to this day," Dimé said. "We spent the entire 2019 aligning as a group," she said. "Now, they all use that six-step process for difficult conversations. And everyone understands the Box of Life concept. I literally took the nuggets and went through them with my team. Our team went through a lot of change, and now I'm hoping for growth. For the first time, we're all speaking the same language."

Today, she continues to work with one of the coaches on our team and then had her entire department learn and review the training.

"It was a life-changing experience for me," Dimé said. "I give credit to my coach. She was my rock, and she still is."

Frank, Tammy, and Dave also saw similar breakthroughs with their problems.

Dave, with his background in the military, learned how to interact on a more personal level with his employees.

For one person, Tom, he left a personal note as a thank you. This was a person who quietly went about his work without much acknowledgment. Dave knew, from working with us, that an employee like Tom is at risk of leaving. If someone doesn't get any kind of feedback—positive or constructive— they may be inclined to feel invisible. Tom was the kind of guy that Dave couldn't afford to lose to turnover. But after leaving the note, he never heard back from Tom, so initially, he thought he didn't make an impact. Then, months later, he spotted the note pinned to the side of Tom's computer. Dave had made the right decision.

"It must have done something for him to hold onto it," Dave said. "I would have never done that in the past."

Frank's problem was he was promoted and became a supervisor, then inherited a conflict between his employees. He had a lack of confidence and knowledge in how to address it. He was quiet and preferred to stay out of conflicts. Using our model to set expectations, Frank worked with his team members and started by working with them to set SMART goals. And it worked.

"Before, I don't think I would have had the knowledge or the comfort to do that," Frank said. "Now I can go in, say what I need to say, and set the expectations."

Tammy's problem was she thought leadership meant having to have all the answers and do all the talking. Now she knows that she has more leadership skill than she gave herself credit for—she's an excellent listener and asker of questions. Her confidence has grown, and as a result, she is more inclined to speak up in meetings. She also uses her new skills in setting expectations and correcting behavior with her foster children ages six, three, and two.

"I would never have been the person to talk first," Tammy said. "Now, I have more confidence."

Problems can come in all shapes and sizes, as we've seen from these examples. They can be navigating conflicts or feeling stuck at work, as in the above scenarios. They can also be

> TAMMY'S PROBLEM WAS SHE THOUGHT LEADERSHIP MEANT HAVING TO HAVE ALL THE ANSWERS AND DO ALL THE TALKING.

problems in operations or with customers. When they persist, they can start to feel overwhelming. But almost all problems are manageable with a deliberate process. Leaders start by defining the statement of the problem, making decisions, and then executing the model. If you have a problem, you can move to solutions, as we'll see in the next action step.

Action Step: Putting Problem-Solving into Practice

CIDER as a process and framework for problem-solving is just the beginning because it's simply a high-level outline of steps for solving problems. So the question now is: How can we actually put CIDER into practice? We have a tool for that.

This is a very versatile tool. It's a tool you can use on your own when coaching another individual through a problem, and even with a group. You can also share this tool with team members to enable them to do problem-solving and decision-making on their own to develop their capabilities. On the following two pages, think about a problem you're currently trying to solve in your work. Fill out the worksheet to help you develop an action plan for addressing the problem.

Another option is to use the worksheet with someone else to help guide them through their own problem-solving process.

You can find this worksheet in your Resource Guide or as a stand-alone worksheet at www.livingasaleader.com/book.

Worksheet for Problem-Solving and Decision-Making

Identify—and briefly describe—a problem you are currently trying to solve in your work.

You will follow the CIDER process below to address your problem.

C   Clarify the problem
I   Identify ideas and possibilities
D   Decide on actions
E   Execute the plan
R   Review and evaluate outcomes

C—CLARIFY the Problem
What's the Current State (problem statement)?

What's the Desired State (goal statement)?

What do we already know about the problem?
List everything we know to completely and objectively unpack the situation.

Sample Questions

- What are the known facts?
- When/where did this happen?
- What have we tried?
- What happened from those attempts?
- What obstacles are in the way?
- What will happen if we don't solve it?
- Who needs to be consulted or informed?
- What <u>don't</u> we know about the problem that we need to know?

I—IDENTIFY IDEAS and Possibilities
What are all the ideas and possible solutions/actions we might consider?

Brainstorm freely. Involve everyone's perspectives and ideas. Don't analyze or criticize.

D—DECIDE on Actions

What are the pros and cons of the ideas and possibilities?

Who will be impacted and how? Who needs to be informed and/or consulted as a result?

Which ideas will we try?

E—EXECUTE the Plan
Who will do what and by when? Who is the final decision-maker?

R—REVIEW and Evaluate Outcomes

What is our follow-up plan?

7

BUILDING TRUST

Bruce was reviewing shipments and customer order reports as his company wrapped up another quarter. It's going to be another weekend of overtime, he thought. Bruce is a plant manager in Tennessee for a large-scale manufacturing company with welders and skilled workers. They work twenty-four hours a day over three shifts and then added extra weekend hours during any given month as needed. He knew this weekend was one of those times. Goodbye, weekend. Bruce knew this especially bothered his team when they had plans to watch football or barbeque. In the South, college football Saturdays are sacred. But what could be done? They had to meet their quota.

Then he received a call that no one wants to receive. Tragedy had struck. One of the plant's beloved employees, Junior, had just died in a motorcycle accident. Bruce rushed out to the scene, just to be there. He stopped thinking about their productivity. Some things are bigger than work.

Junior was the employee everyone wanted. He worked hard out in the shipping yard, often in 90- to 100-degree temperatures, always full on. He was not a time-waster, not a wander-around kind of guy. He was friendly and helpful, likable and positive. As he walked out the door, moments before his motorcycle hit a pothole in the road, he said, "See you tomorrow, boss! I'll bring the donuts!" His last words, most likely, ever spoken.

Bruce knew that this news would devastate his team. He learned that the visitation and funeral would be on Saturday—which was the day for mandatory overtime. In that moment, he knew there was only one thing to do. He gave the entire plant off on Friday and Saturday. Those who knew Junior had to have time to pay their respects and to grieve.

"At the time, it was just the right thing to do," Bruce remembered. "I thought I was going to be in trouble, but I didn't think of the ramifications of it. I reached out to my boss, and he supported me."

At the funeral, Bruce encountered Junior's father. "You shut down the plant for my son," he told Bruce, overcome with emotion.

You shut down the plant for my son.

With this profound and simple statement, Junior's father illuminated the core of leadership: A regard for common humanity. Recognizing that people's needs matter. Doing the right thing at the right time. Acting from the best possible values.

> THE CORE OF LEADERSHIP: A REGARD FOR COMMON HUMANITY.

Afterward, Bruce made sure that counseling and support were available for his team. It wasn't simply about ordering people back to work, even with new pressures and orders mounting. They needed time to heal.

We met with this group of workers after this incident, but it was still fresh in their minds. They were caring human beings, salt of the earth people. It would be fair to say they had never been introduced to concepts like emotional intelligence, intentional leadership, making sure to give people positive feedback, having difficult conversations in a respectful manner, or helping employees sort through conflict. This is an area in our country, just outside Chattanooga, Tennessee, where everyone has an endearing nickname. Rob is "Utah." Jimmy is "Bubba." Jonathon is "Hunter." Rob #2 is "Ripp." They all tend to have a dry sense of humor and tend toward sarcasm and ribbing of each other. When the topic of Junior's death came up, the normally jovial group of tough guys sat in silence, seeming to fight back tears.

What struck us was the level of appreciation these guys shared that day toward their plant manager. It was off the charts. They were beyond grateful. As a matter of fact, they were all still hanging on to a similar incident that had happened ten years earlier, when they were not extended this same courtesy and sensitivity for their natural grieving process. The deceased individual was not important enough to leadership to pause production and goal achievement. These guys essentially said, "The way Bruce handled this has now erased our bitterness for what was done ten years ago." The final sentiments that we remember from this conversation were, "We have a long way to go to heal from this loss. We will never be the same. We will never forget what Bruce did for all of us."

This is what we mean by trust. It's what Bruce did. It's always doing the right thing.

The Importance of Trust

In his classic business book *The Five Dysfunctions of a Team*, Patrick Lencioni paints a portrait of a fictional Silicon Valley company that should be high-performing on paper—has plenty of talent and cash, a large technology and engineering budget—but is losing out to its competition. The talented collection of individuals in the organization aren't functioning as a team, and as a result, are all viewing each other with suspicion, disdain, or lack of faith. They have no trust in each other. That, Lencioni writes, is the first dysfunction of a team. Without trust, there is no foundation to build upon. Everything else falls apart.

"Trust lies at the heart of a functioning and cohesive team," Lencioni wrote. "Without it, teamwork is all but impossible."[15]

Our team member, Rick, learned the importance of trust from the first CEO he worked for. This leader told him that in his experience, relationships based on trust are less expensive. They expend less energy, less time, fewer legal fees, and less aggravation and anxiety. Most of us can describe the benefits of gaining others' trust. We can even describe the behaviors that attract it, including consistency, fairness, honesty, keeping our word, respecting others, etc. Trust is the foundation of effective and enjoyable relationships, workplace or otherwise.

One of our authors, John, characterizes trust as "the immune system of all human relationships." If the trust between us—our immune system—is healthy, we can fight off the inevitable "bugs" that come between us. If our immune system is weak, one little infection can keep us down for weeks.

> IF THE TRUST BETWEEN US— OUR IMMUNE SYSTEM—IS HEALTHY, WE CAN FIGHT OFF THE INEVITABLE "BUGS" THAT COME BETWEEN US.

We've all been part of or seen situations where trust is in short supply. Maybe trust evaporated when employees have felt short-changed once too often. Perhaps trust eroded because leaders were never open to involving their team members in solving problems or open to hearing their points of view about workplace challenges or changes. Or leaders never bothered to get buy-in or commitment from a team to begin with and simply fell back on the authority of titles and positions.

Under good circumstances, with profits coming in, a system without trust can function and do the minimum to get by. Orders and rules can get people to comply, at least for a while. But at the first sign of adversity, teams without trust fall into turmoil. That's when blame starts getting assigned, and resentments simmer back to the surface. Without trust, teams splinter apart at the first sign of a problem rather than coming together to solve it, like they would if they believed in each other.

Building trust is not a gimmick, and it's not a one-time thing. It doesn't come from a team member putting their safety in the hands of their colleagues. (Just search for "trust fall fails" on YouTube to see these well-intentioned exercises go horribly wrong—or better yet, don't.) Instead, trust can only be earned over time by demonstrating that a leader is willing to do the right thing, even and especially when it's not easy. For leaders, building trust is absolutely essential. We have seen talented leaders fail when their teams were not behind them because those leaders didn't build trust.

Nine Ways to Kill Trust

It's true that it takes years to build trust, but it can be destroyed in an instant. Trust can also exist but be eroded by insidious behaviors that leaders may not even know their team is noticing. We have seen leaders fall into these traps. Consider some of the subtle actions that can crumble trust:

> IT TAKES YEARS TO BUILD TRUST, BUT IT CAN BE DESTROYED IN AN INSTANT.

1. Not Playing by the Same Rules

Bruce, the manager you met earlier in this chapter, has to take safety extremely seriously in his manufacturing plant.

He's had to fire employees for being on cell phones on the shop floor or walking under a crane in the plant, both serious hazards. Because he needs to be strict on these rules, he has to abide by them himself. His team looks to him to set examples, or they notice any inconsistencies. So if Bruce goes into a safety zone without safety glasses, missing his hard hat, and talking on his cell phone, his team will see that. He's had to tell his peers and even his CEO to make sure they leave their cell phones behind when on the work floor. "If I had not held him and myself accountable," Bruce said, "how can I hold others accountable?"

2. Not Using Inclusive Language

In *The Five Dysfunctions of a Team*, a new CEO works to bring together a group of individuals that don't function together as a team. At first, she refers to the group as *you*. Then she gets called out on it. To her credit, she immediately sees her mistake and works to include herself as part of the team. To get them acting as if they all belong together, she needed to start referring to *us* and *we* instead of you and me. If the group is really all in it together, start talking like it.

3. Publicly Criticizing Team Members

Problems and mistakes need to be addressed, of course, but this should be in private and through proper channels. It also creates team members that are less likely to be accountable for their own mistakes if their failures will be magnified in front of their peers. Being publicly critical of others breeds an environment of fear and distrust.

4. Publicly Criticizing the Organization

Everyone needs to vent from time to time about their boss, company, or peers. But a leader should never do this in front of their team of direct reports. If a leader doesn't put their trust in their own institution, why should their team trust the leader? As Tom Hanks's character, Captain John Miller, in *Saving Private Ryan* remarked, when challenged by his squad of soldiers that they never hear him gripe, "Gripes go up, not down. Always up." Furthermore, if a leader is criticizing and undermining their own bosses, then are they throwing their team under the bus too?

5. Making Trust Transactional

We once worked with a leader from a military background who never said thank you to his team. His thought process was that he was never thanked for his work since he was just following orders and doing his job. Why should people be thanked for simply doing their duty? Trust, however, doesn't come from a paycheck or a job description. It's not transactional. Thinking that someone will trust you because you're ordering or paying them to do a job may bring compliance but not trust.

6. Not Following Up

One leader that we've worked with had an axiom for good leadership: *Reply to people's emails.* This is meant both literally and metaphorically. No, leaders don't need to reply to every email in their inbox (and often, an in-person response is better). This means, simply, that the team has to know that a leader is responsive, available, and willing to make efforts to follow up and circle back. As we've emphasized before in this book, not checking in with your team to keep them accountable leaves them adrift and uncertain. It does them a disservice not to provide constructive feedback and praise when appropriate. When leaders don't follow up appropriately on a question, a goal, a task, or simply an email, it signals that they can't be bothered to care enough about the outcome or about others. When a leader doesn't make the effort to follow up on the small stuff, can they really be trusted when a project, someone's well-being, or even the company is on the line?

7. Not Following Through

If you want to build trust with people, do what you say you'll do. We realize that everyone is busy, including you. At the same time, when you make promises and commitments to do something, follow through. Reliability breeds trust. Be a person of your word. If that means adding your promise to your task list or calendar to make sure you follow through, do that. If it also means circling back with the other person to let them know you're still working on it and haven't forgotten—especially if unforeseen obstacles or delays come up—do that too. People will respect, appreciate, and trust you for your commitment to your commitments.

8. Being Inconsistent

Have you ever had a leader who was moody or unpredictable? You didn't know which version of the person would show up on any given day or from situation to situation? Such a condition creates instability and uneasiness in the team, and it wears away trust. As Daniel Goleman pointed out through his research on emotional intelligence, in every human group, we look to the leader as our emotional guide. If people can trust that you will show up in a predictable and consistent manner, they will trust you. If you don't, they won't.

> IF PEOPLE CAN TRUST THAT YOU WILL SHOW UP IN A PREDICTABLE AND CONSISTENT MANNER, THEY WILL TRUST YOU. IF YOU DON'T, THEY WON'T.

9. Never Apologizing

We've worked with leaders who thought they didn't need to apologize if they made a mistake. Did that mean they were never wrong? No, of course not. They thought apologizing made them look weak or simply that leaders didn't need to apologize. We all make mistakes, including leaders. Failing to honestly own up to mistakes when necessary makes a leader look inflexible, unfair, arrogant, or self-serving. The only thing worse than never apologizing is a partial apology: "I'm sorry, but . . ." Rather than accept responsibility and build trust, this type of apology only inflames resentments and destroys trust. As Ben Franklin reportedly said, "Never ruin an apology with an excuse."

> "NEVER RUIN AN APOLOGY WITH AN EXCUSE."

The behaviors and actions that we outlined above are quick ways to destroy or erode trust. We don't condone them, of course. They're simply not good practices for building trust as the foundation for engaging your team to deliver results. The opposite of these behaviors is what we need to strive for because trust needs to be built up in a deliberate way over time. If you think about the people you've trusted most, they probably behaved very differently from the erosive behaviors listed here.

Reflection: Trust Models

For Bruce, the plant manager at the beginning of this chapter, his father-in-law provided a model of trust. His father-in-law was a West Point Military Academy graduate with high integrity, and he became one of the people Bruce modeled himself after when he became a leader.

"He was a true servant leader," Bruce muses. "I watched him through the years, how he handled adversity, and how he did not let that affect his relationships."

Deep trust in someone—that they have our best interests at heart—is not something we give out lightly. It's an honor that is earned through time, actions, and intent. But when we put our trust in someone, they become a model to us for how to act for others.

Think of a person from your life that you trust deeply. It could be a parent, a close friend and confidant, a sibling, or a historical figure like Gandhi or Mother Theresa.

What makes this person trustworthy? What words do they say? What actions do they take? What big and small steps have they taken to earn your trust?

Write these qualities down on the next page so that you can incorporate them into your own behavior.

Trust Models

Trust Building

Conflict is going to happen in every organization and on every team. Conflict is natural when humans work together, and when handled correctly, conflict can be healthy and productive. Disagreement is a fundamental way that teams learn from each other, grow, and move forward stronger than before. A key ingredient between productive and unproductive disagreement is, you guessed it, trust.

On teams that don't trust each other, conflict becomes personal, prolonged, and nasty. On teams that have trust and mutual respect, they can disagree and still move forward. It's what Lencioni called "disagree and commit." This paradox is only made possible if everyone on the team believes that the others on their team have their best interests at heart. The highest levels of trust can't be earned simply by avoiding behaviors that erode trustworthiness. It comes from doing the right thing in moments of hardship, crisis, or when it would be easier to simply go with the flow.

Trust can't develop apart from concern and commitment. The bottom line is that we have earned trust because we have behaved in ways that show we care for this person and their well-being. If we are trusted as leaders, it is because we have moved beyond the job description. We have brought commitment and integrity, even when it costs us, to the relationships.

Let's revisit the example of Bruce, the plant manager who earned the trust of his employees when he shut down the plant for a funeral. For Bruce, this was personal. It reminded him of his own experience. He recalled twenty years ago when his mother suffered a terrible car accident. She was in the hospital four hours away, and Bruce thought he had to put his work first. He tried to push down his worry and put on a stoic face at work. Internally, he was struggling, and he did less of a convincing job of hiding that than he thought. Others noticed.

"I put that on myself and took it out on people I shouldn't have. I was feeling bad about myself," he remembers. "It's hard to be on your A-game every day."

When his entire plant was going through mourning over Junior, he knew it would take a toll on them. Even for these tough guys with a hard exterior, they couldn't just push it down and move on. So he acted. He did the right thing. And he earned their trust.

The following week, something surprising happened. The entire plant pulled together. They stepped up. Their output to get the necessary work done improved. In some ways, you could say they did this for Junior's memory. But really, they did it for each other. They trusted each other because Bruce created the environment where everyone could be vulnerable when it was needed.

Time passed, and work continued in the plant. Then one day, Bruce woke up, and he realized something was wrong—very wrong. He ended up in the hospital for nine days as doctors removed a tumor the size of an orange. Bruce lost fifteen inches of his small intestines.

This was a hard position to be in for someone used to being responsible for all areas of a manufacturing plant, from mowing the lawn to profit and loss. And outside of work, Bruce was a weightlifter who relied on going to the gym. Now, he was in the hospital and almost helpless. It was his turn to be vulnerable. He always worked to build trust as a leader. Now, he had to trust his team to work without him.

That's when his team came to visit him, one by one. His production manager came to see him: *"Hey, do me a favor,"* the production manager said. *"Don't worry about work. We've got it."*

"Do you know how much that meant to me?" Bruce said.

The trust that Bruce built up came full circle.

You shut down the plant for my son.

Don't worry about work. We've got it.

A regard for common humanity. Recognizing that people's needs matter. Doing the right thing at the right time. Acting out of your good values. In fact, Bruce's team did perform at a high level while he was out. They earned his trust, which is a two-way street.

Today, Bruce is back to weightlifting and working at the plant, sometimes showing up in the middle of the night to share awards with his third-shift workers. He gets scans every four months for the next five years to make sure he's cancer-free. So far, so good. But this experience has expanded his perspective about what's really important and the legacy that he leaves as a leader.

"As long as I can look in the mirror and say I tried to do the right thing for our company and our guys, then I sleep well," he said. "I sleep well."

Action Step: Your Trust Quotient

So how well does your team trust you? This can be a hard question to answer—people don't usually tell us flat out whether they trust us or not. But we can get a sense of it from the interactions we have with others.

Think about your team members. Which ones do you think trust you the most? How can you tell? Which ones do you think trust you less? How can you tell?

On the next few pages, we took the nine ways to kill trust, and we flipped them into constructive behaviors. Think about someone on your team with whom you'd like to build trust and rate yourself on each of the behaviors. Identify two or three behaviors that you can enhance in your relationship with that person and begin practicing them immediately and consistently with this person and the rest of your team.

One final note: If you need to, make an apology. Your team member will be quicker to trust your new efforts if you share that you know past behaviors didn't express your values and that you are now committed to new ones. And if you apologize, do so sincerely the first time: You can't go back to the "apology well" more than a few times before it loses all effectiveness.

Stick to your new behaviors for the sake of your integrity and the potential for trust to be regained.

My Trust Quotient

1 = Never, 2 = Rarely, 3 = Sometimes, 4 = Often, 5 = Always

1. I follow the same rules I hold this person to.

    1 – 2 – 3 – 4 – 5

2. I use "we language" when talking to this person.

    1 – 2 – 3 – 4 – 5

3. I speak positively about this person in front of the team.

    1 – 2 – 3 – 4 – 5

4. I speak positively about my boss and other parts of the organization in front of this person.

    1 – 2 – 3 – 4 – 5

5. I show gratitude toward this person.

$$1 - 2 - 3 - 4 - 5$$

6. I follow up and circle back with this person.

$$1 - 2 - 3 - 4 - 5$$

7. I follow through on promises I make to this person.

$$1 - 2 - 3 - 4 - 5$$

8. I am consistent in how I approach this person.

$$1 - 2 - 3 - 4 - 5$$

9. I apologize to this person when I make a mistake.

$$1 - 2 - 3 - 4 - 5$$

8

RESOLVING CONFLICT

Think back to a time you had a conflict, and in the end, you discovered you were wrong all along. Lucky for you, the other person acted patiently and reasonably during the process. The problem was you couldn't see their perfect logic and correct way of doing things staring you in the face. Because of your stubborn belief that you're always right, you reacted irrationally with terse emails, defensiveness, and frustrating avoidance, all the while dragging out the problem and making it worse. You made this other innocent person's life miserable.

Finally, you realized—maybe years later—that you could have handled the situation better. As the saying goes, "Never ascribe to malice that which is adequately explained by incompetence," also known as Hanlon's razor. Another way of saying it is, "Never ascribe to malice that which is adequately explained by not seeing the full picture."

Have you ever had this moment of insight? The sinking feeling where you realized you had egg on your face?

In a conflict, we see the other person as acting irrationally. That's because we can't help but see things from our perspective since we're the one who is inside our head. We have the full picture of ourselves for context and understand our justifications. As we discussed in the Box of Life exercise, in our mind, everything we do is rational and has an explanation. Even if we admit that something is partially our fault, we understand why we acted the way we did, given our history or state of stress or the circumstances we were under. Our behavior makes sense to us, even if it seems baffling to others. And besides, our intentions are always good. Right?

This may come as a surprise: The person you had a conflict with likely felt the exact same way about you—that you're the irrational one. This is the root of conflict and why it can be so difficult to resolve. But to come up with conflict resolutions, it takes an open mind to rise above this mentality of only seeing things our way.

In some ways, conflict is at an all-time high in our society, aided by thought bubbles in social media and partisan polarization. According to a Pew Research study in 2020, about nine-in-ten Americans (91 percent) say that partisan conflicts are either strong or very strong. About seven in ten (71 percent) say these conflicts are very strong.[16] This contentious environment indicates a deeper root issue: It's easier to view other people as the problem rather than deal with underlying disagreements.

Here's an example of two people we worked with who had a conflict, and both of them saw themselves as doing the right thing. Names and details have been changed to protect their identities.

Jack is a leader, and Jill who reports to Jack, is a compliance officer. As with all conflicts, there are two sides to their story. As you might imagine, both see themselves as right. One of our coaches, Rick, worked with these co-workers. First, he assessed the situation and heard each side of the story. Rick didn't intend to "play King Solomon," an all-wise coach who assigns who's right and who's wrong. Instead, Rick worked to help them understand the layers underneath that caused their conflict.

"It's easy to just say, 'Knock it off,' but guess how effective that is?" Rick said. "We first have to understand the problem."

According to Jack, Jill didn't manage meetings in a way that made the amount of content digestible to the entire team. In addition, she gave too many unnecessary details, which slowed down his fast-paced drive for results. In essence, Jack felt Jill could be a more effective meeting facilitator.

According to Jill, Jack didn't communicate information accurately or thoroughly given his active, off-the-cuff communication tendencies and lack of attention to details. She thought, *He just wings it and is happy with everyone getting the gist of the message.* He didn't seek her out as the content expert to help him. She also thought he didn't support her decisions, given his tendency to change the direction of meetings from her talking points to his.

This conflict was ultimately self-destructive. Both felt that the other didn't want to be helpful or need the other. Jack fell down, and Jill came tumbling after.

Here's the catch: Two people can both be right in a conflict. And often they are. People have good reasons for their behavior—and their opinions. We all have unique tendencies for how we deal with situations, and we all bring opinions and perspectives. As the saying goes, the "truth" lies somewhere in the middle.

The problem comes when our approaches are at odds. The problem is heightened when we're not willing to hear the other side sharing rational explanations for their tendencies, preferences, or actions. We want to see ourselves as 100 percent right and them as 100 percent wrong. So how do you get past that mentality? In this chapter, we'll explore the steps that lead to understanding conflict and handling conflicts with sustainable conflict resolutions.

Conflict Happens

The presence of conflict doesn't mean failure. In fact, conflict is often helpful in coming up with the best solutions. To use an analogy, friction is necessary to produce a spark. But too much friction creates gridlock. It's the leader's job to help manage conflict so it doesn't reach an unhealthy or counter-productive level. A leader can help others through conflict and handle conflict constructively.

One thing all leaders need to first recognize is the reality that conflict is going to take place. It's not a question of if; it's a question of *when* and *how*. There isn't any long-term relationship that doesn't experience conflict at some point: It happens in families, it happens in marriages, it happens in friendships, it happens in politics and government, it happens in partnerships, it literally happens everywhere.

Conflict is a natural response to different and competing styles, needs, and priorities. When managed correctly, conflict can even be healthy. For leaders, when conflict comes—and it will come—it will be key to understand why it happens, and if possible, how it can be resolved.

We know it when we see it, but conflict can take many forms. It doesn't have to be outright hostility, yelling, and fighting. Conflict can look like the petulant defiance of a teenager, with plenty of eye-rolling, ignoring directives, and being slow to act. Conflict can be passive-aggressive, with a whisper campaign spreading rumors and putting up barriers. Conflict can also look like compliance, with people saying one thing to your face to look like the model employee but doing another thing in private or in other situations. Conflict can be sarcasm, disrupting meetings, stonewalling, defensiveness, or a reply-all email that is meant to undercut authority. Or conflict can just mean a stalemate, without anger or ill-will. There's no shortage of ways that conflict can manifest.

Reframing Conflict

Conflict is one of those words that seems to trigger everyone who utters it or hears it. Humans seem allergic to conflict. We often ask leaders to do free association to the word conflict when we first start talking about it. The usual terms they come up with are words like fight, disagreement, tension, and anger. Once, a leader freely associated to "conflict" with: "No, thank you." It's not a word or idea that is pleasurable to us. Could it be that we don't understand it? Or have pre-conceived notions about it from our past?

The ability to stay calm and respond productively to conflict is a hallmark of an effective leader. In fact, research shows that a leader's inability to effectively manage conflict will lead to negative outcomes and also undermine the credibility of the leader.[17] Unfortunately, one of the most common shortcomings of a leader is the inability or unwillingness to resolve conflict. We often have at least one conflict going on at any point in time, and the most common response to conflict is avoidance. Leaders avoid dealing with conflict between others and (as humans) avoid dealing with their own conflicts (flight) or handle them in a way that makes them worse (fight).

> THE ABILITY TO STAY CALM AND RESPOND PRODUCTIVELY TO CONFLICT IS A HALLMARK OF AN EFFECTIVE LEADER.

Many leaders, because of their lack of skill in this area, will fall back on clichés like, "You need to play nice in the sandbox." This is code for "I don't know how to help you." Conflict resolution is a critical skill area that needs to be developed and practiced as conflicts arise before the impact escalates. Avoidance almost always adversely affects the metrics related to retention, engagement, productivity, and profitability. This is why we have training and workshops around the idea of resolving conflict.

We want to help leaders move from avoidance or mishandling of conflict to handling it productively, with confidence and with competence, whether the leader is a party in the conflict or needs to mediate it for others.

We define conflict this way: **Conflict is a disagreement that escalates to a point that you can't move forward productively.** This is likely how we all think of conflict, but social psychologists tell us that there are really two types of conflict. One is considered healthy and useful and helpful, and the other gets us into trouble. Knowing the difference can help us navigate to productive conflict and away from the problematic type.

> CONFLICT IS A DISAGREEMENT THAT ESCALATES TO A POINT THAT YOU CAN'T MOVE FORWARD PRODUCTIVELY.

1. **Cognitive Conflict**. You might think of this as healthy debate or discussing issues or problems (conflicts) in a calm and thoughtful way. Cognitive conflict occurs when people have different opinions on important issues and are willing to discuss various perspectives, hear each other, and co-create a solution. This type of conflict and way of managing it is the one we consider "good" conflict, and it's an approach we encourage and foster. It is an approach to conflict that makes it easier to solve the issue productively.

2. **Affective Conflict**. The one we usually think of, which is messy and emotional, isn't very productive. This type of conflict is more personal in nature. Affective conflict shows up as emotional escalation. It's adversarial. We often become personally attacking with this type of conflict. It is disruptive and creates stress for other members of the work team. It can lead to

disengagement and lack of buy-in and commitment. Affective conflict may show up through tone of voice, body language, silence, raised voices, and accusations.

In reality, what defines the type of conflict we're having (affective or cognitive) is in the approach we take toward the fact that you and I disagree on something. It's how we choose to address it. Conflict itself is not the problem. How we handle it is. The trick is to be able to take an emotionally charged conflict and move it to the cognitive place, whether you're in the conflict or mediating it for others. That's why our mediation approach, which we'll share with you in this chapter, works so well—it's a cognitive approach to an emotionally charged situation that allows for us to share perspectives, listen to each other, discuss options, and problem-solve together.

Do we take an affective approach and get all worked up, or do we take a cognitive approach? One way to stay on track with a cognitive approach to conflict is to remember that there are four common sources or reasons for conflict. We call them "situational drivers" of conflict.

1. Personal Issues (different communication styles or backgrounds, personality clashes, people who simply don't like one another)

2. Infrastructure Issues (layers of leadership, reporting relationships, unclear roles and responsibilities)

3. Limited/Lack of Resources (computers, budget, space, people)

4. Unclear Expectations (about performance, behavior, information, deliverables)

No matter the source of conflict, they can all lead to the same result if not managed effectively: Discord, disharmony, and a loss of productivity. Historically and consistently, conflict is often referred to as a key factor that contributes to decreases in productivity, trust, communication, engagement, retention, and morale in the workplace. If managed ineffectively, conflict results in significant cost, turnover, increased absenteeism, and more. At the same time, when managed effectively, conflict can produce positive outcomes like heightened innovation, improved productivity, stronger relationships, and higher performance. Study after study has shown that conflict is pervasive among employees, and about a third of employees encounter conflict either frequently or always.

> CONFLICT IS OFTEN REFERRED TO AS A KEY FACTOR THAT CONTRIBUTES TO DECREASES IN PRODUCTIVITY, TRUST, COMMUNICATION, ENGAGEMENT, RETENTION, AND MORALE IN THE WORKPLACE.

Unmitigated conflict has a cost. According to Michael Segovia, senior consultant at The Myers-Briggs Company, employers in the US pay $1 billion each year due to workplace conflict, managers spend 20–40 percent of their time responding to employee conflict, 2.8 hours per week are spent by individual employees in dealing with conflict, and workplace conflict is a decisive factor in more than 50 percent of employee departures and in over 90 percent of cause-related terminations. That's a huge drag on the bottom line.

Regardless of the type of conflict, we can all benefit by pausing, then planning a response. It only makes matters worse to react quickly and emotionally to a conflict without thinking through the repercussions of our own actions. Instead, we can maintain a list of proactive ideas to handle conflict that offers an alternative to the more natural tendency of an aggressive or passive-aggressive, negative response. This is treating conflict as cognitive rather than affective:

- Take a deep breath

- Talk through the conflict together

- Seek areas of potential agreement

- Express ideas and feelings in a neutral way and urge others to do the same

- Offer solutions and encourage others to offer their own

- Focus on the facts, not on emotional reactions or things you have heard through the grapevine

- Discuss expectations in the beginning

- Disagree with ideas, not the person

- Be quick to forgive

- Legitimize others' feelings without agreeing

The list above may sound like common sense, but each suggestion requires thoughtful commitment and application to become common practice when faced with a conflict situation. When we work with leaders, our first step in resolving conflict isn't to jump to solutions or decide who's right and who's wrong. It's to recognize the conflict, define the type of conflict, and understand why it's happening. You can't fix what you can't understand. So, let's take that first step together.

Reflection: Recognizing Conflict

In this reflection, pick a conflict that you are currently facing or have recently faced. Then select one of the four situational drivers for conflict that we just talked about (personal issues, infrastructure issues, limited or lack of resources, unclear expectations) or a combination of the four as applicable. Then reflect on the following questions:

Recognizing Conflict

1. Briefly describe the conflict situation.

2. What have you tried so far to resolve this conflict?

3. Which of the four situational drivers are at play in the conflict?

4. What is the biggest barrier to solving this conflict?

5. What is one productive thing you think you could do to make progress in resolving this conflict?

6. What specific benefits will you gain by learning to handle this conflict in a more productive manner?

For the last step, it may seem like common sense that we'd want to handle the conflict in a productive manner. And yet we often get sucked into the drama of a conflict, hold grudges, and stoke the fires of outrage long after the moment has passed. That's a natural response in the heat of the moment, and we don't always respond to conflict in a manner that will be productive. That's why we have to remind ourselves that a productive resolution is actually the goal and will bring further benefits.

Sticking to a Plan

Mike Tyson famously said that everyone has a plan—until they get punched in the mouth. A conflict can feel like that uppercut to the face that has you seeing stars or seeing red. It can make you reactive rather than proactive. That's why it's so important to be able to explain and understand conflict and then be able to practice and fall back on steps to resolve the underlying issues. As a leader, when mediating conflict between others, we provide steps for resolution via a Mediation Meeting Planner.

This planner is based upon a mediation model that was originally developed by John Rutkiewicz, a member of the Living As A Leader team and co-author of this book. Our goal in sharing this planner is to provide you with a consistent, comprehensive way to resolve conflicts as productively as possible. And it can also work when you are dealing with a conflict of your own.

This Mediation Meeting Planner incorporates a key concept within transformative mediation, a leading school of thought in mediation. The concept is that there are two interpersonal conditions that you, as the mediator, are striving to stimulate and create during mediation—*empowerment* and *recognition*.

In conflict, it's crucial that you let each party tell his/her story in an open environment. This stimulates empowerment that the person's voice and perspective are valuable and need to be heard. Conflict tends to leave us feeling weakened and threatened, so empowerment is about helping each of the two parties feel strong and secure about themselves.

The steps in the planner also encourage and support the parties in listening, being receptive, and restating what they hear. This stimulates recognition—"I understand your point of view and acknowledge it as valid." Conflict tends to drive us into self-absorption, so recognition is about helping each of the two parties be responsive and open to the other.

By focusing on both empowerment and recognition during conflict, you are in effect taking a cognitive approach because the process tends to de-escalate and neutralize emotions that could get in the way of resolution.

The Mediation Meeting Planner uses the following seven steps:

Mediation Meeting Planner

1.	WELCOME AND PURPOSE	Sample Language: • Thank you for agreeing to attend this meeting. The purpose of the meeting is to engage in a dialogue about (conflict topic) and work toward mutually agreeable solutions.
2.	MEETING AGENDA	Sample Agenda Items: • Agree to ground rules • Establish individual objectives for the discussion • Discuss roles in the process • Create dialogue to achieve shared understanding and resolution
3.	ESTABLISH GROUND RULES	Sample Ground Rules: • Speak from your own experiences—unique perspectives, opinions, and feelings about the situation • Share factual information—be open and honest while speaking factually • Listen deeply—no interruptions, seek meaning and feelings behind the words • Maintain confidentiality—do not share information or perspectives outside this discussion ASK: Do you agree to these ground rules? What other ground rules would you like to add?

4.	CREATE DIALOGUE	Sample Language: I'd like to begin the discussion with three questions to establish your individual objectives and set the stage for a deeper discussion in a few minutes. (Ask each participant one at a time) • How do you feel about being here right now? • How have you been feeling about what's happening between the two of you? • What is one thing that must happen today for you to feel that this meeting was successful?
5.	EACH PERSON SHARE STORY/ EXPERIENCE	Steps to Use: • Have one person start by sharing their experiences related to the conflict • Encourage the other person to ask questions for clarity • When the first person is done, have the other person restate in their own words what they heard that person say—get agreement • Repeat the first three bullets for the other person • Work toward agreement

6.	WORK TOWARD AGREEMENT	Steps to Use: • Ask participants to brainstorm possible actions/behaviors that may help resolve this issue (flipchart) • Ask participants to individually choose from the list which actions/behaviors they will focus on to contribute positively to resolving the issue • Ask participants to share their action items with each other • Give participants an opportunity to ask for a specific action/behavior from one another and gain agreement
7.	CLOSE THE DISCUSSION AND FOLLOW UP	Steps to Use: • Ask each participant to share closing thoughts on this meeting • Ask each participant to send you individual action commitments • Mutually agree to a time to get back together for follow-up and to discuss progress

This plan to handle conflict may seem formulaic, and that's exactly the point. Remember the quote from Mike Tyson: Everyone has a plan until they get punched in the mouth. The goal is to stick to the plan, even when those blows start to land. At the same time, resolving conflict should also have a human element and acknowledge emotions without succumbing to them. For example, you might not do a meeting agenda and ground rules, but jump in at step five to learn the other person's point of view and feelings, share your own, brainstorm together and work toward agreement, and summarize and follow up. That's why this planner incorporates facts, empathy, other-centeredness, and accountability. These are the cornerstones to effective communication as a leader in the face of all different types of challenges.

In the action step for this chapter, you will have an opportunity to apply the Mediation Meeting Planner to a current workplace conflict situation. But first, let's revisit Rick's situation with Jack and Jill to see what happened in their stand-off conflict.

Jack and Jill Work Together

Recall from earlier in this chapter the situation of Jack and Jill. Jack thought that Jill was too detailed in her meetings and was not presenting information in a concise and digestible form. Jill thought that Jack was being too superficial and simply "winging it" in meetings with his team. He wanted to move fast, and she wanted to be careful. The more one of them pushed and asserted their style, the more the other person pushed back. These differences in approaching problems led them not just to disagree on style but also resent each other as people.

Rick, who worked with them both, started by meeting with them individually to establish the facts of what was causing their conflict—their different styles. Jack was a get-it-done fast kind of person, and Jill was more cautious and thoughtful in her approach. On that, they agreed. But they also each got something out of the conflict. It allowed them to feel righteous anger, see themselves as the hero of the story and the other person as a villain. They could even build alliances against the other person. The only problem is they were ultimately hurting themselves by corroding the team and the company from within. So how did Rick defuse the situation?

"You have to connect to a person by meeting them where they are, and you can't be judgmental, or you won't be effective," Rick said. "You have to use questions rather than give them answers. You have to let them come to their own resolutions. We ask questions to get people to think. I'm not there to solve problems for the leaders I work with. I'm there to help them figure it out."

For the next step, it wasn't about determining who was right or wrong, or even getting them to like each other. It was simply about coming to an agreement that would work for both of them. That ultimately would serve both of their purposes by helping the business both of them worked for. Ultimately, managing their conflict was about achieving a business outcome, not just creating harmony between colleagues.

So together, they discussed their situations, shared their perspectives, and laid out an agreement. Along the way, they also listened to each other to better understand.

Jack agreed not to interrupt Jill, even if he thought she was going into too much detail in a meeting. Instead, he would make a note and discuss it with her later offline. No more interruptions in meetings.

Jill, for her part, agreed not to "flood" Jack with details but to provide key bullet points to save time. She would also provide feedback later, privately, if she felt he wasn't listening and had tuned her out.

They also both agreed that, after group meetings, they would follow up individually with each other to ensure alignment while playing to each of their strong suits. In their own conversations, they would state the intention for their meetings, such as setting expectations for information sharing or decision-making. They agreed to create a shared agenda for structured meetings and ensure written action items as the next steps.

Notice that by setting clear expectations, defining the goals, and setting up a process for enforcing their shared agreements, Jack and Jill set up a way to interact with mutual respect. In this way, Jack and Jill can go up a hill together—and stay there.

Action Step: Using the Mediation Meeting Planner

In this exercise, select a current workplace conflict that two of your employees are having with one another. Select a situation where you can help resolve this conflict by having a mediation meeting with these individuals. Use the Mediation Meeting Planner as a template to prepare for and conduct the meeting. Alternatively, if you don't have a situation with others but a conflict of your own, use the planner to plan out how you'll have that conversation.

Remember, practice your plan so you can use it. Steer toward using the cognitive approach. Always keep in mind that conflict doesn't have to be a nasty drag-out issue. Recognize that it can simply be a situation where people or teams don't seem to be in alignment about an issue, process, or situation, but they can work through it to reach a better situation.

You can download blank copies of this planner at www. livingasaleader.com/book.

Mediation Planner

1. Welcome and Purpose	
2. Meeting Agenda	
3. Establish Ground Rules	
4. Create Dialogue	
5. Each Person Share Story/ Experience	
6. Work Toward Agreement	
7. Close the Discussion and Follow Up	

9

NAVIGATING CHANGE

When he first started making pizzas, Giacomo Fallucca worked out of a garage. Pizzas were all simple and handmade. There were maybe half a dozen styles. It was a small, family-owned business that grew out of his father's vision to make and provide food to others. In the 1960s, the family business started as a bakery, then a restaurant, and finally Palermo's Pizza, which opened up in 1979, baking frozen pizza. Not much changed in those early years. Pizza was cheese, sausage, or pepperoni. That was it.

"We started everything by hand," Giacomo remembers. "We were scrappy, and we focused on local suppliers."

Fast forward to today—and everything about the food industry has transformed. Complexity has skyrocketed. Today, it's not uncommon to go to the grocery store and see dozens of varieties and brands for even staple foods like beans, sour cream, or even a carton of milk. (Do you want skim milk, 1-percent milk, 2-percent milk, whole milk, goat milk, raw milk, organic milk, chocolate milk, strawberry milk, lactose-free milk, almond milk, rice milk, hemp milk, flax milk, hazelnut milk, coconut milk . . . you get the idea.)

Now multiply those changes by all the ingredients and styles that could make up a pizza. Just the crust alone could be thin, medium, thick, pan, deep dish, Sicilian, New York-style, Chicago-style, Detroit-style, Neapolitan, authentic wood-fired, focaccia, flatbread, gluten-free, sweet potato, cauliflower, or hemp, just to name a few. There are websites and blogs devoted to breaking down the different types of pizza crusts. That doesn't even begin to describe the toppings variety.

Marketing has also changed. Early on, Giacomo's father could rely on the restaurant's reputation spreading through the neighborhood by word of mouth. Then as they scaled and grew, they could reach thirty media markets through three TV channels. Making a commercial on one of those channels could reach the whole country. Now trying to reach someone means finding them somewhere between Facebook, Instagram, Twitter, LinkedIn, Snapchat, YouTube, newspapers, magazines, advertising flyers, direct mail, e-mail marketing, network television, cable television, Hulu, AM radio, FM radio, SiriusXM radio, Pandora, Spotify, Apple Podcasts, or countless other digital channels.

Today, Giacomo runs the business out of a building called Palermo Villa in Milwaukee's Menomonee Valley. The 250,000 square-foot facility is modeled after the authentic style of an Italian village, complete with a research and development kitchen, expansive employee dining room serving a pizza buffet, and corporate boardroom decorated with pizza boxes. When walking by the building, the delicious aroma of fresh tomato sauce drifts down the street, along the river, and near the Milwaukee Brewers' baseball stadium.

As the company has grown, Giacomo no longer knows everyone who works with him. In the early days, he would personally interview everyone who was hired in the company—he wanted to leave his influence and stamp everywhere. But growing and evolving means change. It means he has to train leaders to take over specialized aspects of research and development, production, engineering, packaging, marketing, quality control, accounting, and all other areas of the business.

The game has changed. To succeed, the leadership needs to change too.

Future Tense

> Change is the process by which the future invades our lives.
> —Alvin Toffler, writer and futurist

Change brings with it lots of things: fear, excitement, stress, new opportunity. Plus, change is a very common human experience. We hear common phrases

> "CHANGE IS THE PROCESS BY WHICH THE FUTURE INVADES OUR LIVES."—ALVIN TOFFLER, WRITER AND FUTURIST

like, "Change is all around us." And, "The only constant is change." This seems to be increasingly true in this fast-paced, complex world that we find ourselves in. Change is just a part of life. In one of our workshops, Support Yourself and Others Through Change, we explore the dynamics of change, discuss resistance to change, and identify how leaders can be better at helping themselves and coaching others as they navigate through change as effectively and efficiently as possible.

A vast majority of the research on change management comes from a strategic, organizational viewpoint—how to plan for and structure large-scale change initiatives. Yet, in our experience working with leaders and organizations over the last twenty-plus years, we've seen how important it is for individual leaders to be better at helping people understand, accept, support, and embrace change. You can have the best, most grandiose change initiative in the world, yet if the people who need to implement the change aren't on board, how can it succeed? The bottom line is, people are the primary factor in the success or failure of any change effort.

PEOPLE ARE THE PRIMARY FACTOR IN THE SUCCESS OR FAILURE OF ANY CHANGE EFFORT.

For a leader, the key to success during times of significant change is to minimize the depth and duration of lost morale and productivity that commonly come with change. To accomplish that, the leader must acknowledge and address the predictable reactions to change. Leaders must, in fact, expect resistance. So often, leaders respond to resistance with intolerance, impatience, and frustration. Ironically, that slows down others' acceptance of change. Rather, by acknowledging and addressing resistance early and often, the leader will help increase the likelihood of readiness for and acceptance to change. Employees want to feel acknowledged and understood.

Some sort of change in an organization is going on at any given time, either internally or in the external market, that contributes to the success of an organization. Internal changes may relate to restructuring, new technology, quality improvement, new products and services, new leadership, retirements and succession, cost-cutting measures, and cultural renewal—you name it. Externally, market globalization, stiff competition, regulatory upheaval, and explosive digital technology also contribute to a destabilizing environment. Some companies adapt and thrive, such as Amazon, Google, Apple, McDonald's, Starbucks®, and Netflix. Other companies and industries have not adapted well, including Blockbuster, AOL, GM, and shopping malls.

Consider the following recent statistics:

- The average organization has undergone five enterprise changes in the past three years. Only one-third of the change efforts are clear successes; 16 percent show mixed results, and half are clear failures. (Gartner, 2019)

- Change-stressed employees perform 5 percent worse than the average employee. This performance decline translates to a $32.5 million-dollar cost to the bottom line per $1 billion in revenue. (Gartner, 2019)[18]

- In the 2018 Talent Development Research Report *Change Enablement: Skills for Addressing Change*, 92 percent of respondents reported that their organization underwent a change in the past three years, and only 19 percent indicated their organization was highly effective at addressing the change.

- The primary reason change fails is that management behavior doesn't support the change, and employees are resistant. In essence, people are the primary factor in the success or failure of any change effort. The organization doesn't change until people change. (McKinsey and Company, 2015)[19]

Change Models

There are two key models to keep in mind in order to be more effective at leading change. One is the Rational Change Model. The other is the Emotional Change Model.

All successful organizations go through a predictable evolution. We call it Rational Change, which applies to whole companies, divisions, business units, departments, and even teams and workgroups. There are three phases of these changes in a company:

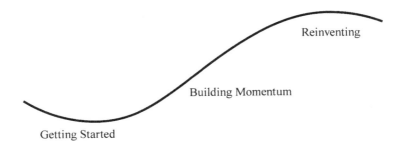

Getting Started is an entrepreneurial phase. It reflects a time of high energy, creativity, financial investment, and sweat equity with little formality or infrastructure. Think of Giacomo running the small, family-owned business out of its first small facility.

Building Momentum is a growth phase. It reflects a time of increasing maturity, organization, structure, addition of formal leadership, and profitability. Think of Giacomo opening a new factory with 700 employees and launching new pizza styles.

Reinventing is a transformation phase. Reinventing—combining old ways with new ideas—is essential for the life of any business. Think of Giacomo deciding how he's going to continue innovating through new pizza styles while growing the company.

Let's explore each of these phases in a bit more depth.

It's important to note that change can happen at any level or size in the organization, from full company to a small workgroup or any size in between, such as a department or division. Leaders can be responsible for leading change no matter where they find themselves within the organization. In the Getting Started phase of an organization—or of a business segment, or even within a new team—there is a great deal of creativity and trial and error taking place. This is often referred to as the entrepreneurial phase in which there is little formality or infrastructure. This is also the time in which spending typically exceeds revenue. Courage and risk-taking are needed to advance an organization toward success. Do you have a segment of your organization that is in a Getting Started phase?

As time goes by, an organization eventually moves to the next phase, Building Momentum. Here, organizations experience profitability, efficiencies are established, procedures get put into place, and much growth occurs, both in terms of employees and overall success. This phase in the evolution of organizations used to, in some situations, last decades. A risk for many organizations is that they become "fat and happy" during this stage. Complacency can set in as well, and there becomes a tendency to "do what we have always done." Organizations will indeed get into trouble if they stay in this phase too long. The Building Momentum phase will reach a point in which they are either changing or dying.

All organizations typically evolve to a point in which it is critical to ongoing success that the organization "reinvent" itself. Reinventing is the third phase in the Rational Change Model. The Reinventing phase represents a time of innovation and creativity. This is the time when organizations challenge the status quo and make assumptions about what is best. During this phase, organizations often develop new products and services or enter new markets for versatility and continued growth. This is a blend of the old with the new. Within organizations, we have employees who are trying to preserve the past, while other employees are very ambitious about change. By continuously reinventing themselves, companies ensure their own organizational sustainability.

Sell the Problem

Ultimately, leaders need to convince others why change is needed and renewal is required. Leaders need to demonstrate why change is needed to keep growing, get better, or remain competitive. The Rational Change Model provides us, as leaders and businesspeople, with a framework by which we can explain and understand the rational reasons for change. What thriving, reinventing companies and teams do is constantly look for ways to change to improve their business and operations and take advantage of new opportunities. In fact, in the smart companies, they don't wait until their Rational Change Model is beginning to take a tumble before they launch anew. By continuously reinventing themselves, leaders ensure their own sustainability at all levels of the organization.

Examples can help demonstrate the problems and solutions that change can bring. Amazon, for example, is a model of continuous reinvention. What did Amazon first sell when they came into the marketplace? Books. Now what do they sell? Everything. When Jeff Bezos started Amazon, that was his plan all along—to build the world's largest online mall that sells just about everything. That's why it was called Amazon—like the vast Amazon River.

Selling the problem is helping people understand the why of the change—the problem we're trying to move away from. Susan Bridges, an author and expert on organizational change, put it:

> Make sure that the statement ties the change to the existing situation that makes the change important. Sell the problem before you try to sell the solution. Don't try to make a change to meet a challenge, solve a problem, or seize an opportunity until you establish this in people's minds.[20]

The Rational Change Model allows leaders to both under-stand the mindset of their team and then, more importantly, be able to use that model to communicate the need for change— what we typically refer to as "sell the problem." The benefit for leaders is to be able to demonstrate the need to change. Selling the problem enables people to understand the real why behind the change and to remove their attachment to the past, which can prevent their willingness to move forward.

Reflection: The Rational Change Model

Now, let's bring this model to your team level. To summarize, the lesson of the Rational Change Model is that organizations, departments, workgroups, and segments throughout will move through a predictable evolution, and they will need to con-tinuously change in order to survive and thrive. The same is true on your team. Leaders at every level play a central role in the successful implementation of changes, both big and small, within the segment of the organization that they lead. But first, you have to discover what phase of the model is driving change within your team. Note that you will likely be in all three phases in different ways at any one time. Your team may be bringing on a new team member (getting started), refining a procedure that needs to work better (building momentum), and brainstorming a new service or product (reinvention). All of these activities bring change, and all of them are intended to solve some sort of problem.

On the following page, think about your team right now, identify examples within each area on the Rational Change Model, and get clear on the problem that change is intended to solve.

Your Team and the Rational Change Model

What are examples of Getting Started in your team? What are the problems those changes are striving to solve?

What are examples of Building Momentum in your team? What are the problems those changes are striving to solve?

What are examples of Reinventing in your team? What are the problems those changes are striving to solve?

Managing the Emotions of Change

The Rational Change Model is useful to help us effectively lead change in our teams and organizations, but it isn't enough. In fact, in a lot of organizations, leaders stop at understanding and communicating change only from a rational, problem-based perspective. Yet, change also brings out a great deal of emotion. Regardless of our rational reasons for organizational change, people generally respond emotionally when change occurs. It is a predictable human reaction when coping with change. We make decisions about whether changes are good for us or bad for us based on our emotional responses.

Now we're going to turn to that other important side of change—the emotional side. As McKinsey and Company reported, "People are the primary factor in the success or failure of any change effort." Dr. Jerry Jellison at USC put it more bluntly: "The fundamental problem of implementing change . . . is people's emotional resistance."[21] Looking at the rational side of change is important, but for leaders, it is even more important to focus on the human side of change.

To start, think of your own experiences in life: What are examples of significant, *positive* personal or professional changes you have experienced within the past couple of years? Did you get married, have kids, buy a house, get promoted, or find a new job with a great company? Brainstorm these positive changes in the space below.

```
┌─────────────────────────────────────────────────────────┐
│                                                         │
│                   Your Positive Changes                 │
│                                                         │
│                                                         │
│                                                         │
│                                                         │
│                                                         │
│                                                         │
│                                                         │
└─────────────────────────────────────────────────────────┘
```

With these positive changes you've had, what did you lose? Next to each item you wrote, write down what you had to give up.

Even with positive, often self-created changes, we experience loss. Loss and endings are at the core of all change, even the ones we consider "positive." Given that, it is no wonder why people struggle during times of change within organizations. And it's also no wonder that for decades, more than two-thirds of change efforts have failed.

As MIT Sloan School of Management professor Peter Senge wrote: "People don't resist change. They resist being changed."[22] Loss and endings are at the core of all change, and with loss come other predictable human reactions—feelings of confusion and uncertainty, a desire for self-protection, drops in productivity, and less teamwork and collaboration. With all of these predictable dynamics of change present in organizations, people often wonder why change needs to happen at all, and yet, as we've talked about already, change is necessary for growth. Our goal is not to think we can eliminate change. Rather, the goal is to figure out ways to navigate ourselves and others through change as effectively and efficiently as possible, given that, for humans, change is a highly emotional process. The Emotional Change Model helps to understand why that is.

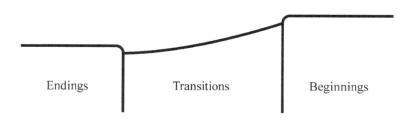

As changes take place in organizations, people typically go through an emotional process. Our Emotional Change Model mirrors the three phases described by William Bridges[23] and further draws from the field of *transition psychology*, which studies the emotional and psychological stages humans often experience when confronted with change. The Emotional Change Model illustrates what happens on the human side and the impact of change on individuals throughout the organization. There are three distinct stages to the Emotional Change Model. They are the Endings stage, the Transitions stage, and the Beginnings stage. We are going to look at each stage and discuss characteristics, emotions, risks, and communication needed in each stage, along with important action steps for you to take as a leader when your people are in each stage.

Every change begins with an ending. When something changes, it marks an ending of the past, an ending of the old way. Often, these endings are difficult for people. It's not unlike dealing with the loss of a loved one or a prized possession—or dealing with the losses that came with the *positive* changes you described above. On the opposite side is the desired destination of the change—the new beginning, the other side. The intent of change is to get to a better way. In between Endings and Beginnings is a gap. This is what we call the Transitions stage between the old and the new. Across this gap spans a rope bridge, which is unstable, shaky, high up, and potentially dangerous.

According to Bridges, anytime we encounter a change, we must go through each of these three stages in order to be able to accept the new way. Sometimes the journey is a quick one in which we're immediately on board and ready to go. Sometimes we get stuck in Endings, unwilling or unable to let go of the past. And other times, we find ourselves lost in Transitions, not sure whether we want to return to the old way or embrace the new.

This model provides us with a framework for understanding the different stages that people go through as they react and respond to change emotionally. As people, we all react to different changes in different ways at different times, and a group of people who are affected by a change may individually be at different stages at the same time. This model helps us understand why our standard, rational approach to change in organizations, by itself, often doesn't work to bring people along emotionally.

A Change Scenario

Let's look at a scenario that illuminates the model. Usually, when a change takes place in an organization, it doesn't just magically happen. It's a long process. Consider the following example: Let's say that we're a part of a group, such as a taskforce, to develop a plan for change. One day, early on in our taskforce, Joe presents an **idea** in our taskforce meeting for the potential change. We don't think much about it at the time, but a month later, Joe brings it up again. We start to **talk** a little more about the idea. As we talk more and more, we really begin to **like** the idea. We put together a plan to **explore** the idea by doing a little field research. A couple of weeks later, we present the idea to the executive team, and they give our change project the green light—it's a **go!**

From there, we spend several weeks working to **develop** the ins and outs of the change idea; we do some **tests** to help perfect our plan, then proudly, just last week, we are ready for **LAUNCH**. We announce the change and introduce the idea to the organization.

Now, consider this: For those of us on the taskforce, where are we on the Emotional Change Model at this point? *Beginnings*. The taskforce members have been involved since they first had the idea months ago. They've had months to move through the Emotional Change Model and get ready for the change up until the time it's rolled out. Those on the taskforce are gung-ho!

And where is the rest of the organization when we first introduce the project to them? The rest of the organization, for the most part, is at *Endings*. We often don't do enough for the majority outside the change initiative to ready the organization for change. If we're the decision-makers or otherwise involved in development of the change, we don't consider that people also need to move through an emotional process of letting go of the old so they can embrace the new.

Communication throughout the change process becomes an important consideration. Typically, the way in which we communicate with people during times of change is dependent upon where WE are in the Emotional Change Model. People in Beginnings want to be inspirational and convey the "rah-rah" kind of message (like our taskforce might). They'll try to "sell the mountaintop" of the great new world we'll have with this change, and they forget to sell the problem to take people back to the very start of where the change process began. The trouble is, the person you are communicating with is not ready for that stage. They are in Endings. So, if we are already at Beginnings and talking with someone in Endings, the risk is that we will convey impatience, intolerance, and lack of recognition when others need to deal with the loss of Endings.

There can be a real disconnect and hurt feelings when people don't realize they are in different stages. A colleague of ours once worked with a vice president who called together the office to announce she accepted a new position at another company. At this point, the leader was in Beginnings and was excited for her next move. But her team at that moment was still absorbing the shock of the news. The room was silent, and the meeting ended on a quiet and somber note. The vice president seemed genuinely confused at the reaction. "Well, is anyone going to congratulate me?" she asked, sounding hurt, as the meeting broke up in stunned silence.

Here's another brief story about that: A member of our team was employed at one time by an organization that was going through a significant, enterprise-wide change initiative involving loss of jobs, change in jobs, buyouts, different products, and many other changes. When this very controversial and painful change initiative was announced by senior management, they were at the Beginnings stage of the Emotional Change Model. They had spent months already personally going through Endings and Transitions. They were on board and had figured everything out. They were ready to move ahead. When they made the announcement to the management team of 300 people, they were like cheerleaders! They said how great it would be, that it wouldn't be that bad, that it was about time, and that people need to just get on board.

People were devastated, shocked, stunned, sad, and debilitated. Because the 300-person management group was largely in Endings at the time of the announcement, the senior managers should have shown empathy, support, and provided as much information as possible behind the need for this change. Instead, they became intolerant and unable to relate to the concerns.

Communicating During Endings, Transitions, and Beginnings

With this story as a backdrop, let's talk about the communication needs for people when they are in the Endings stage. In this phase, give people in this stage a chance to talk about the past, what they'll miss, what they're unhappy about, and their concerns. Be empathetic, supportive, encouraging, and listen. As the leader, you need to walk over the bridge to their side, be with them there at Endings, and patiently help them to get ready to begin walking to the other side. If you don't invest the time and empathy into these actions now, others will take longer to accept and embrace the change, and success will be delayed or unachievable.

Given time and encouragement, those in this stage can eventually move to the Transitions stage. People at this point may ask a lot of questions, appear upbeat and optimistic one day and struggling the next, or they may be stalled by unanswered questions or feel overwhelmed, curious, or anxious. In this stage, leaders need to be informative, educational, and clarifying. The call to action for the Transitions stage is to sell the problem (the reason for the change). Leaders should reiterate information on the problem we're trying to solve with this change. This approach often helps to keep people from going backwards to the old way. The perceived pain of the old can be a motivator for movement toward the new.

Finally, people whose emotions have reached the Beginnings stage have accepted the change. They are ready to take on whatever new assignments are necessary. They are open to adjustments in their role, and they recognize that things will not be the same. Some people move across the bridge quickly, almost instantaneously, to arrive at Beginnings. Others may take much longer to get here.

Those in the Beginnings stage will look the part. They will appear enthusiastic, have high participation, be productive and engaged, and serve as team players and change leaders. But there are also risks involved, including intolerance and lack of empathy for others who aren't coming along as fast or alienation of others who don't share their enthusiasm. At the same time, they can be faking it! This is a risk of "Yes Man" syndrome, where they appear to be on board but don't really follow through because they don't believe in the vision.

The call to action for people at the Beginnings stage is for you to show tolerance and to ask for tolerance from them. It's important for you to show tolerance for those who are at Endings or Transitions so you can help them move toward acceptance of the change and so that you can support their journey to get there. The early adopters, if tolerant of others, can also be great assets in helping others accept the change. For example, they can provide training and guidance to others to help them cross the bridge.

Change by the Slice

Giacomo is an extremely high-energy guy. When he's telling a story, he leaps out of his chair and runs around the table to illustrate his point. He talks a mile a minute, peppering his conversations with questions. He asks others about their favorite books, their day, their team. He appears to be someone who's perpetually in the Beginnings stage, ready to race off to the next start line. He likes to win.

"A lot starts with my father," he said. "I saw what he did. He had no fear about where he wanted to go. When he saw something, he immediately saw what it could become. He was racing 100 miles an hour towards the goal. For me, I also see what things could become."

After we worked with Giacomo, he came to realize that not everyone is always going to be in the same stage as him. He can't clone himself or recreate the small family company. And that's okay with him. He knows that to grow the company and scale, he needs to surround himself with different personalities and skillsets. That also means leading people through the Transition stages to get to the next change.

"If I look at my style, I have a high sense of urgency, low patience, and I always wanted people who had that same fire in their belly," he said. "Now I recognize that's not just going to be the case at all times. That's the reality of teams and leadership. It's just how it is. I recognize the differences."

When the team was a small group of *pizzaiolos*, change happened more quickly. There was little time between Beginnings, Transitions, and Endings. One of the company's first home runs of innovation was primo ultra-thin crust pizza with restaurant-style toppings, back when that was rare in the grocery freezer. They devised the idea, and then it was executed.

"That was the extent of our research," Giacomo remembers. "That was it."

But now, the marketplace is much more complex, and innovation demands a more thoughtful plan with many more people involved. A grocery store chain may call up Palermo's and ask for twenty-seven different varieties of pizza. The company has to decide if they can even handle that kind of production. Now innovation has to be wrapped in data and complex consumer preferences. Gut feeling needs to be balanced with adequate research and layers of execution.

"There used to be two people doing innovation, and now there are twenty-five—quality, procurement, manufacturing, packaging, engineering, etc.—and that's kind of bureaucratic," Giacomo said. "But that's the reality of the company because of the size. I don't want to be small. I want to be large. The leadership training helps to run our business in a way that evens out the gaps. Leadership is what helps to make sure people are prepared."

Around the time we first met him, Giacomo was working on a new type of pizza inspired by the craft beer industry's attention to detail, premium ingredients, and bold branding. It featured an in-your-face packaging with a gaping mustachioed mouth that opened to reveal the ingredients inside. The names for these new pizzas included Mother of Meat!, Bessie's Revenge Loaded Pan, Lucky Clucker Stromboli, and their newest, 'Za Brewski, a collaboration beer-infused pizza. The new line was a sensation.

"It was a market disruptor," Giacomo said proudly. "I thought we knew every available supplier in the Midwest and U.S., the best sauces, cheeses, toppings. We could make it in a hand-tossed way, and we could do it better. It's a craft-produced locally sourced pizza with hand-touches. We were putting on slices of mozzarella by hand. XYZ pizza company couldn't hold a candle to us in terms of flavor. We were the ultimate craftsmen of pizza."

Now it's approaching a decade since this pizza line, Screamin' Sicilian, became the new guy in the frozen foods aisle with "an attitude big enough to make a grown man cry." Since then, the competition for new styles, new flavors, and new innovation has become even more fierce. Giacomo's company has also changed. The small, family-owned business now has 700 employees and produces a staggering 300 styles of pizza. *Pizzaiolos*, as the company's workers are called, may change the type of pizza they are working on every hour over the course of the twenty-four hours that the factory is open each day. It takes a lot of coordination, patience, empathy, and leadership to help the team advance to the next frontier.

When asked what he's most proud of in his forty years leading the company, Giacomo said it's that he's been teachable. He listened to others. He changed. Giacomo is a big fan of Frank Sinatra and his anthem "My Way"—but he said that only captures part of what he's done in the company.

"I did it my way," he said, "but I also brought in and listened to others."

He paused.

"But that wouldn't have made as good of a song title."

Action Step: Applying the Emotional Change Model

Now let's have you personally apply the emotional impact of a difficult change. Think about a change at work that's impacting you right now, one that you are struggling with or haven't fully accepted yet.

On the next pages, answer the series of questions to examine the change that you're experiencing through the lens of the Emotional Change Model and to plan your next steps.

Navigating My Own Change

1. What is the change I am thinking of?

2. What stage am I in regarding this change?

3. What can I gain by supporting the change?

4. What if I don't go along with the change?

5. What one to two strategies can I implement to minimize my resistance and move toward Beginnings?

6. What support will I ask my leader to provide?

7. How might I benefit if I implement my strategies and seek support from my leader?

10

THE LEGACY OF LEADERSHIP

When we introduce the concept of leadership development to people, there are generally two strong reactions to taking personal responsibility for growth and development. Either people embrace it, or they resist it. They may go into their leadership journey with their eyes open, seeing the value in how they can get to the next level as a person and a leader. They may bristle at the idea that they could be doing something wrong, or they simply may have a blind spot to their effectiveness in leading others. We've seen plenty of examples in both camps.

When we met JP Moran, we knew immediately he belonged in the first example of a leader—he was hungry to learn. He was humble, eager, and coachable. JP was a model student who was also going back to school at the time to earn his MBA, where he sat in front and participated frequently. His professors often looked to him to share real-world examples with the class. JP didn't know it at the time, but he was building a legacy of leadership for himself and his family.

JP would also admit that he was an unlikely leader, at least at first.

In 1967, JP's grandfather created a small label-making company in the back of a Chicago butcher shop. Label Makers, Inc. continued to quickly grow and soon extended beyond the Second City. Nearly twenty years later, JP's mother, Jean, took over the leadership of the company as CEO. Jean worked to transition the company into LMI Packaging Solutions, a strong female-owned and operated business. LMI grew significantly and added locations in multiple states.

At the same time, JP had no interest in taking the reins. For her part, Jean encouraged JP to find his passion and never pressured him to take over. Finding his own path meant earning a kinesiology degree and becoming a high-end personal trainer in Chicago.

"I never wanted a part of it, and I didn't want to deal with food packages," JP said. "Plus, I didn't like the stigma of a family business." He didn't want people to think he was just handed his position due to the coincidence of birth.

Becoming a personal trainer, in many ways, was exactly what he needed at the time. This role inadvertently helped prepare JP for relationships in business. He learned how to listen, how to motivate, how to hold people accountable, and how to be direct when needed. Above all, it taught him how to empathize. JP realized that being a personal trainer is one of those professions—like a bartender or hairstylist—where you become a part-time therapist. People tell you everything, and you realize that everyone is always going through something they may not show on the outside. Clients sometimes broke down in tears between sets. He had his own Box of Life as a personal trainer.

"I saw when people had an emotional breakdown," he said. "It's an emotional thing when you build a relationship with people on that level."

As he approached the end of his twenties, however, he found himself seeking something more. He wanted to take the people skills he learned one-on-one with clients and apply them to a setting where he could have a larger impact. His job wasn't challenging to him anymore, and he wanted to find meaningful work. So he came home. He started over.

Going back to his family company, JP started in sales. Still, the stigma he feared seemed to come true, at least in his mind. But there was no other way than to confront it head-on and lead by example.

"When I first started here, I was considered the 'spoiled momma's boy,' and it was hard to hear that," he said. "But sometimes you just got to dive in and keep working. Then you hear that less and less."

This was around the time when we first met JP for leadership development. JP participated in our year-long leadership development series, a combination of skill-building workshops and leadership coaching sessions. He was eager to learn and better himself. And it worked. After two years in sales, he moved up to become a shift lead in his company. After nearly a year in that role, he became a national account manager. Then he spent more than three years as general manager. Finally, he moved into the role of company president. He kept learning at each level.

As JP saw it, he had to keep bettering himself to become polished and professional. The only way to remove the stigma, as he saw it, was to work extra hard to show people that he was worthy of the title of leader—not because of his last name.

> THE ONLY WAY TO REMOVE THE STIGMA, AS HE SAW IT, WAS TO WORK EXTRA HARD TO SHOW PEOPLE THAT HE WAS WORTHY OF THE TITLE OF LEADER.

All the training was helpful to build his confidence and skills. He proved his bona fides. He proved he belonged. But ultimately, he realized that he didn't need to keep trying to prove a point. Leadership isn't about the leader.

"I thought I was far behind," he said. "Then I realized it's not all about the knowledge and growth. It's about the people."

At first, JP didn't want anything to do with leadership. But as he learned—and as we've seen through several examples in this book—it's never too late to develop a legacy of leadership for yourself and for others. As a leader, you can find meaning in your work in any industry because it's ultimately about your impact on people.

> IT'S NEVER TOO LATE TO DEVELOP A LEGACY OF LEADERSHIP FOR YOURSELF AND FOR OTHERS.

Finding Meaning

Every generation wants their work to matter. For many members of the younger generation, work is central to their identity. JP is on the older cusp of the millennial generation. Like many in the workforce of his generation, he went off exploring and followed his first passion before dipping his toes into a new direction and career.

A report from Gallup titled "How Millennials Want to Work and Live" shows how millennials are altering the very social fabric of America and the world. Defined by their lack of attachment to institutions and traditions, millennials change jobs more often than other generations—more than half say they're currently looking for a new job. "Millennials will change the world more decisively than any other generation," says chairman and chief executive officer of Gallup, Jim Clifton.[24]

Millennials don't just work for a paycheck—they want a purpose. Millennials are not pursuing job satisfaction—they are pursuing development. Millennials don't want bosses—they want coaches. Millennials don't want annual reviews—they want ongoing conversations.

Millennials don't want to fix their weaknesses—they want to develop their strengths. And, one of the most important discoveries: Millennials don't just see work as a paycheck and a means to an end—to them, it's their life. One of the hallmarks of this generation of workers is they deeply want to see meaning in their work. They want to find their passion. They want their impact to matter.

While hanging out in Colorado for a couple of days one holiday season, one of us, Aleta, had a casual conversation with a young professional couple who happened to be sitting next to her in the lodge. Let's call them Liz and Patrick. Both were millennials. It was interesting to listen to the things that matter to them. And the things that are potential deal-breakers.

The summary of Liz's story: "I am thirty-one and the oldest of our sales team. My boss is twenty-eight, and she's awesome. She knows how to lead. She leads five of us, and she is really good about helping us learn the things that she's done to be successful so early in her career. She meets with us individually every Monday. She has mentored us on how to generate leads, how to have conversations with people we've never met, how to adjust our style to our audience, how to track our opportunities. She holds each person on our team accountable for progress, she is available to help us when we need it, she joins us on sales calls, entertains prospects with us when it's important, and then she stays out of our way."

Liz's boss's boss, the VP of sales, however, was very challenging. Liz elaborated: "The VP of sales swoops down (uninvited) and inserts himself into our opportunities with no interest in learning about the opportunity, the prospect, or the situation. He sends emails and text messages directly to our prospects because he thinks we need him to advance the deal and, ultimately, close the deal. He shows up at prospects' offices unannounced; he over-talks during sales calls with these prospects and asks questions that we already know the answer to. It is worth noting that his emails, subject lines, and text messages usually have typos in them. The most recent subject line said, 'Out progress to date.' When I have asked for time to meet with him to brief him on opportunities, a common answer is, 'I don't have time for that. We'll just figure it out as we go.' When I tried on one occasion to talk with him about the ways in which he participates in my opportunities and the concerns I have, his reply was, 'Listen, I've been in sales for thirty years. I don't need you to tell me what to do or how to do it.'"

Patrick, meanwhile, found himself to be very fortunate working for a company that challenged and motivated him in new roles after six years. "After working in a role that I did not find particularly fulfilling, the company took a chance on me and moved me to an entirely new function," he said. "When I got engaged to Liz, who lived across the country from me, they were willing to move me, allowing me to work remotely. Now I am working on interesting projects as a project manager and have access to my leader whenever I need. I don't envision going anywhere soon."

We can all learn something from these examples and the next generation of workers. But you don't need to be a millennial to want to leave a legacy. You just need to think about your vision for yourself and your impact. What do you want your team to say about you? What do you want to be remembered for? What do you want to leave behind? Do you want the world to be a better place in some way through what you contribute as a leader?

WHAT DO YOU WANT TO BE
REMEMBERED FOR?

These questions matter to us. When the two of us (Nancy and Aleta) started our company in the field of training and development, we would essentially create any training program or solution that a company wanted. But over time, we narrowed our training,

192

concepts, and principles to what matters most and what creates the greatest impact—that is effective leadership.

LEAVING A LEGACY THROUGH LEADERS IS OUR ULTIMATE GOAL.

Leaving a legacy through leaders is our ultimate goal.

Reflection: Write Your Legacy

There's no better way to focus yourself and determine what you want out of life than by considering your limited time here on earth. Death is a topic that pertains to us all, and we all benefit when we contemplate our legacy from time to time.

There are techniques to snap ourselves out of our daily routine and consider our larger mission and goals. A public display called the Before I Die Wall is a global art project that helps passersby reflect on their mortality and what matters most. It encourages anyone to write on a mural what they want to do with their life. Another way to reflect is at a Death Café, where people gather to eat, drink tea, and discuss death. It's a franchise of cafes that put a twist on the traditional coffee shop. Instead of wasting time on your laptop at a Death Café, you contemplate your own mortality. To date, there are nearly 5,000 Death Cafes around the world.

The Death Cafe format was started by Jon Underwood, who quit his job in London to spread the message of living life to the fullest by thinking about death. His movement exploded to more than a dozen countries with more than 1,000 gatherings. In a tragic twist of fate, Underwood died suddenly in the summer of 2017 from a brain hemorrhage caused by acute promyelocytic leukemia. His death was unexpected, or as unexpected as can be for someone who thought about death frequently. His leukemia had not been diagnosed. He was forty-four and the father of two children.

In a message on DeathCafe.com, Underwood's wife Donna Molloy reflected on the meaning through the pain. "He lived every day reflecting very consciously on the fact that none of us know how long we have and focused completely on being present in, and making the most of, every minute," she wrote. "We all know this on some level and try and act accordingly, but it's so easy to forget. Easy to lose sight of the bigger picture and get caught up in the minor detail. He pulled off that challenge so many of us can only aspire to, of truly appreciating what we have. This was how he lived his life, and through his work, he helped so many others to live this way too."

"You know you have a certain time left, and then the question is, *What is important for me to do in that time?*" Underwood said in 2014.[25] "That's different for everyone, so talking about death, for me at least, is the ultimate prioritization exercise." When we forget that, we stop really living our lives.

For this exercise, try to write 200–500 words in the third person that reflects on your accomplishments, what you stand for, and your legacy as a leader—both at work and beyond in your other roles. What would others say about you? What would you want to say about yourself?

My Legacy

The Gift of Leadership

When JP was a personal trainer, he came into work one day, and there was an eviction letter on the front door. Apparently, the gym owner he was working with wasn't paying his rent. JP faced a dilemma. He had clients coming for their early morning workout and no place to train them.

JP thought fast and contacted the landlord. The landlord agreed to allow him to use the gym but only on the condition that JP took over and ran the operations of the gym. JP agreed, and he was able to continue in business. It wasn't a responsibility he wanted, but he learned that he was able to step up, solve problems, and help others get what they needed. He learned the value of leadership through that unexpected setback.

When he became the president of his company, he again learned the value of leadership for others—this time for his mother. When he started back at the company business, he could tell that his mom wanted to retire and leave. But she also felt compelled to continue on the family business. She was stuck.

But now that JP worked his way up, learned, and grew into his current position, he's given his mom peace of mind. She can retire, pursue the rest of her life, and know that she has left a legacy that JP will now carry forward in his way, representing his family. For JP, being a leader isn't just about making packaging for food. It's about doing something meaningful for family and people he cares about and carrying the family legacy forward.

"It's been meaningful to have her get out and do the things she loves," he said. "It's a gift."

11

LEAD AND LEARN

Where would you go if given a month to spend anywhere in the world?

If given a choice, Caroline would parachute out of an airplane and drop into a local culture. It wouldn't matter where, as long as it was new to her. Give her enough currency to get her started, and she would find her way and figure it out. Caroline's plan would be to immerse herself in the culture and see how much of the local language she could pick up. She's gone on a similar adventure before, minus the parachute part. When she was in the Navy, Caroline backpacked around Europe for a month with nothing but the uniform on her back and an extra uniform to alternate when she washed her clothes in the sink each night. To her, the thrill of the unknown was the joy of the journey.

"Some of my most enjoyable travel experiences have been, 'Well, I'm here now—better figure it out!'" she said. "You're there for the journey."

Ephraim would want to visit Africa. Working for his family company, he spent years traveling Asia and living in Hong Kong before returning to the United States. Now, he's onto his next adventure, helping manage his company's team in

London. Even as he travels to another country, he wants to keep exploring, and Africa has been on his mind.

"Then you have to deal with all the uncertainty and figure it out," Ephraim said. "And at the same time, that's fun."

Jessie would want to break up her month in different places in the world that would expose her to new cultures, from Phuket, Thailand, to Shanghai, China.

"I would want to get the experience and exposure to a new culture and work with a different set of values," she said. "I really value the differences in people."

This question—*where would you go if given a month to spend anywhere in the world?*—is a fun thought exercise about how you see adventure, the unknown, and personal growth. Notice that no one said they would want to hang out in a motel in a neighboring town. Even though that trip would be easy and convenient, it wouldn't offer anything new, exciting, or interesting. It wouldn't expand your horizons, introduce you to new perspectives, and enrich you as a person.

> WHERE WOULD YOU GO IF GIVEN A MONTH TO SPEND ANYWHERE IN THE WORLD?

Hopefully, you see the metaphor for leadership. Like adventurous travel, leadership is a constant journey that exposes you to new people and beliefs, new challenges and situations, and new experiences and rewards. It's also a journey that keeps going. No one takes a life-changing trip and then declares that they're just going to stay home for the rest of their days. New experiences give rise to new experiences.

> LIKE ADVENTUROUS TRAVEL, LEADERSHIP IS A CONSTANT JOURNEY THAT EXPOSES YOU TO NEW PEOPLE AND BELIEFS, NEW CHALLENGES AND SITUATIONS, AND NEW EXPERIENCES AND REWARDS.

Caroline, Ephraim, and Jessie are all leaders who manage others and have gone through our leadership development series. Caroline's responsibilities included training nearly 100 leaders in her company. Jessie was teaching leadership workshops in her global business before she even had a team of her own. And Ephraim has traveled the world for his family business. Each of these leaders was already a skilled and talented person before we started working with them. Like the best leaders, they recognize that they can continue to grow. Living as a leader is an ongoing process.

Reflection: How Far You'll Go

We've all come a long way.

One way to see the potential in where you can go is to see how far you've already come. If you've already proven that you can grow in your career, why stop now? And it's never too late to reinvent yourself.

Looking back at our own quarter-century together at Living As A Leader, we're grateful for the opportunity to have made positive differences in people's lives. We're proud of helping companies succeed and providing livelihoods for so many families. Looking back at these accomplishments and milestones along the way reminds us of what we're capable of and how our journey takes time to unfold.

At Living As A Leader, we have a Monday morning stand-up meeting every week. It's a lightning round of sharing what we did over the weekend, along with the priorities for the coming work week. In a steady-progress-over-time fashion, we've learned wonderful things about our team members. We've learned who they are and what makes them tick. This weekly practice of ours also serves as a reminder that life unfolds in days and chapters, and we need to pause and take stock of our progress—even on a busy Monday morning.

In this reflection, take a moment to write down some of the most meaningful milestones and accomplishments of your career. While new job titles and promotions may come to mind first, think of the quieter moments when you received a note, an email, or a word of affirmation or gratitude from someone you impacted. Think of the projects where you went above and beyond and the times you proved something to yourself and everyone around you. Think of the days you felt most fulfilled even if you were busy and stressed. Especially think of the times you overcame fear and self-doubt.

After writing down these bullet points, read over them and see how far you've come. And recognize that you've earned it.

Your Career Milestones

Do It Afraid

While we are able to feel pride and accomplishment in our work at Living As A Leader, there have also been some difficult days in our company and in our personal lives. We've had fear of the unknown and worry about the next steps. We've taken chances, unsure of where it would lead. When we started working together, two of us (Nancy and Aleta) were warned time and again not to go into business together. Partnerships can be risky, and if we had a falling out, what would happen to our business? What would happen to our clients and our livelihood? We did it anyway.

If we had listened to the warnings, we wouldn't be where we are today. The two of us are very different people. The fact that we bring different strengths and perspectives to our work allows us to work with many types of people across many different industries. It also means sometimes there were difficulties and differences. But each time that happened, we learned, we continued on our journey, we grew as people, leaders, and partners, and we always arrived at the best outcomes for our employees and for our clients.

Teleportation hasn't been invented yet. There's currently no way to get to your destination by snapping your fingers, just as there's no way to wake up one day and find yourself in the corner office with all the leadership skills you'll ever need. Leadership development is not teleportation; it's transformation. In transformation, we have to go through the tough times, along with the easier times.

Everyone's timeline on this journey is different, and it takes as long as it needs. Reflecting on our own journeys, Aleta worked on and earned her master's in adult education and organizational science over seven years while juggling working as a leadership development facilitator, a part-time consulting gig (before it had a cool name like "side hustle"), and raising three kids. Nancy spent seven years earning her bachelor's and master's degrees while working three jobs, supporting herself as a young adult, and discovering what her true passions were.

Drawing upon Nancy's expertise in designing curriculum, Nancy and Aleta developed programs for nearly every training need imaginable in the early years of our business together. Then, after about seven years, we retired almost all of that curriculum so we could specialize in leadership development. We branded ourselves as Living As A Leader. We brought John on board a few years later, after he had served for decades as a leader, facilitator, and coach in the corporate world. We added more facilitators and coaches and other functions over time as the business grew. Were those long and winding roads? Yes. Was it what we needed to learn to arrive at where we are today? Absolutely. We believe all of us build our success—personally and professionally—one experience at a time.

To stay with the journey metaphor a bit longer, every travel experience is going to require some uncomfortable moments and difficulty. There is a risk. You might encounter delays or unexpected cancelations. You could get lost, find yourself bumping into dead ends, or lead others in the wrong direction while you're figuring things out. The ride could get bumpy.

Leaders who decide to take the leadership journey have a choice: Resent the inconveniences that slow down or change your journey or expect that the journey may be difficult . . . and adapt. Social researcher and professor Brené Brown calls the process of leaning into the discomfort *embracing the suck*. When we work with others, we use a phrase with a similar message: *Do it afraid*. Yes, you may be apprehensive or even fearful of new situations. Do it anyway.

Brown rose to fame in a TED Talk that discusses the importance of vulnerability, and she has since continued to expose the topics of shame, empathy, and courage. She talks about how she isn't immune to her own feelings of inadequacy or imposter syndrome, despite all her credentials and viral moments. But she counsels that it's exactly these feelings that allow her to empathize and connect with others. As Brown writes in her book, *Dare to Lead*:

> "You can't get to courage without rumbling with vulnerability… If you're going to dare greatly, you're going to get your ass kicked at some point. If you choose courage, you will absolutely know failure, disappointment, setback, even heartbreak. That's why we call it courage. That's why it's so rare."[26]

She does it afraid.

Doing something afraid means you also recognize the fear in others, but you help them overcome it. You recognize that anxiety is normal, but you can help equip others with the tools to help them succeed. This was the case with Chris, the president of an insurance company that was facing major changes as it approached its seventieth year in business. For decades, the company had seen modest growth and little change. Then suddenly, business accelerated into high gear, which produced rapid growth. Chris was able to oversee the growth of the team as it grew—until one of the key leaders moved on and left a gaping void in the company's management structure. It destabilized the entire team, and the fear of the unknown was palpable.

"It became really apparent that a smart investment in the future was necessary," Chris said.

The response wasn't to simply replace one all-star with another all-star, which could leave the company vulnerable to sudden changes. Instead, we helped Chris broaden their leadership base and equip many more people who previously didn't see themselves as key players in their own organization. The idea was to open more people's eyes to their own potential. This, in turn, would reduce the fear and uncertainty across the organization and make their future more stable.

"Those anxieties are natural, but if well thought through, they can pretty easily be overcome," Chris said. "People realized they could step up. They took it seriously. It was fun to watch people take their skills and use them in a professional way with some hands-on coaching and development."

Chris watched with pride as the investment in personnel led many people to take their careers to a new level. There was more company-wide buy-in, enthusiasm for responsibility, and willingness to take on challenges. It was empowering.

"It definitely reduces the stress level when you can confidently trust others and let others own their work," Chris said. "I have more confidence without knowing every detail. That willingness changes the game from, 'Do as I say,' to 'This is what we do.'"

This is what happens when you do it afraid. The pay-off can be seen for both the company and the new leaders who step into their roles. There's no guarantee that vulnerability will immediately lead to greatness. In fact, we usually fall on our faces (maybe a few times) before we find our footing. But without daring greatly, without doing it afraid, without saying yes despite not seeing the entire staircase, you'll never put yourself in a position to experience something new. That's the journey of leadership.

Take Your Time

If you take one lesson from this book, here's a big one: Leadership development takes time. In fact, it *needs* time to sink in. Everyone reading this right now has no doubt been to a daylong or morning session of leadership development. These big extravaganzas pump you up, get you motivated with charismatic facilitators, and then . . . you go back to work and move on. We call this the one-and-done method. Research shows that we usually retain only about 10 percent of what we learn in a single sitting. But if we recall and practice these lessons over time, our retention and application go up exponentially. That's why our leadership development initiatives are delivered in a "steady progress over time" way. The same material could be delivered more quickly with a "firehose" method. But just like getting blasted with a hose, most of it splatters everywhere, and you end up with a mess.

> LEADERSHIP DEVELOPMENT TAKES TIME. IN FACT, IT NEEDS TIME TO SINK IN.

To go back to Caroline, Ephraim, and Jessie from the beginning of this chapter, we are still working with them. Their journey is still ongoing. They're learning as they lead.

Caroline has had an incredibly varied background, simultaneously studying English literature with a focus on Shakespeare along with STEM and leadership curriculum. She became the first woman from the U.S. Commonwealth of the Northern Mariana Islands to graduate from the Naval Academy. Her wide-ranging experience includes everything from Surface Warfare Officer in the Navy to business decision consulting for the Girl Scouts, and she added another adventure as a member of Atlas Improv Company, making up four shows on the spot, every week. Now she's responsible for training a team of 100.

When she took her current professional role, she inherited a system with incredibly high turnover. Bringing Living As A Leader in to develop leaders was initially met with extreme resistance. It was dismissed as the "flavor of the month," no doubt by those who had tried one-and-done methods but then saw daily routines revert back to normal. Caroline encouraged people to simply try the methods. What did they have to lose? Then we followed up with coaching to hold people accountable and reinforce the training. And over time, bit by bit, an evolution began to take hold.

Caroline recalls that one production manager, who was a hard sell on leadership development, is now making sure all his people get to workshops and coaching. This was an individual whose management method was to simply tell people to change and then got mad when they didn't. Now he stops, listens, and asks questions. He sets up one-on-one meetings with Caroline to follow up. Change happened.

"Some of those are tough customers who you think wouldn't, in a million years, think about the pillars of accountability," Caroline said. "But because they're in coaching and that holds them accountable, they have to actually use it. I can think of a couple of leaders, in particular, who we have seen really big changes in. They have gotten recognition that they aren't just phoning it in."

Jessie realized through her leadership development journey that she had been taking a "do as I say, not as I do" approach with her own team. Through working together, we identified ways she can communicate, delegate, trust, and then follow through. She is a very results-driven individual and previously preferred to do everything herself. That way, she knew it was getting done the way she wanted it done—but that didn't allow for any growth for her or anyone around her. Now she understands better the differences in people, how they approach work, how they complete work, and how they want to be led.

"I think after the first class, I was like, 'Whoa, this actually applies to me,'" she said. "I had previously trained managers on how to do this, but I wasn't implementing it into my own management style. I am now able to set expectations, follow-up appropriately, and gather feedback and next steps when needed. I have given my team a lot more freedom while also increasing productivity. Applying it as a manager has been difficult, fun, exciting—it has been eye-opening."

Ephraim comes from a family-owned business that includes his father and his brother. In many families, no one ever teaches you how to handle disagreement or conflict—you often just find your way through it. The stakes then become even higher when you introduce a business and ask for a return on investment into that familial setting. Traditionally, the company has operated by a shoot-from-the-hip, entrepreneurial style.

For Ephraim, leadership development has given him the tools to navigate these relationships and roles at work. He's especially benefited from our resolving conflict session, which teaches participants to expect conflict. He's also learned techniques for meeting management, where he can designate formal professional roles for each person. They've created systems in place rather than simply falling back on informal familial roles.

"Conflict is going to happen," Ephraim said. "This has given us a way to handle it by a system, rather than giving up. I've learned a lot in that way. I've grown up with the company, so I was never introduced to this training. We have the intuition, but we were never given the structure. Now this gives you confidence that comes with the structure."

Caroline, Ephraim, and Jessie all have different backgrounds, they have different needs in their current roles, and they all require different tools and training to get where they're going. But they have one thing in common: They're on a leadership journey. So are you.

Final Reflection: Where Are You Now?

As we said at the outset, developing good leadership takes time, dedication, and practice. Throughout this book, we've invited you to think about and act on a wide array of leadership skills and strategies. We've asked you to see people as people, listen, get feedback on your leadership, be a coach, ask better questions, set clear expectations, help people through change, and finally think about your legacy. Though we near the end of this book, the leadership journey continues. It's a lifelong pursuit that never ends until you step off the path.

As this leg of your journey nears completion, it's time to check in on your willingness and skill level as a leader, as they stand today. On a scale from one to ten (ten being highest), answer for yourself these two questions:

At this point in your journey, how willing are you to be a more effective, competent, and confident leader? What's your number? Write it down below.

What's your current level of ability (skill level) as a competent and confident leader? Write down your number.

Compare these numbers to your benchmark from the introduction. Through this book, has your willingness to grow as a leader decreased or increased?

In addition to your willingness, how's your skill level as a leader now? Higher or lower? As we work with leaders, it's not uncommon that their growing awareness of the skills they need to lead effectively leave them feeling, at some point, like they have more to learn than they thought. While this awareness can feel disheartening, as they continue the work, their skills grow and strengthen. Their competence and confidence grow as they practice their leadership skills. How would you rate your skill level right now as compared to your benchmark score in the introduction?

Before we take any journey, it's good to know where we're starting from. These numbers give you some sense of where you are now. On the following page, reflect on how far you've come—and where to go next.

Where are you now?

Action Step: Planning the Next Journey

Research shows that one of the most enjoyable parts of travel is simply planning your trip. Yes, the process of booking flights, making hotel reservations, and creating itineraries can actually be one of the best parts of the journey. Why? Because it creates anticipation, a powerful emotion that signals that the experience is just beginning. It shows that the adventure is a process that unfolds with distinct stages, rather than simply a place to be dropped into. Dreaming about where you will go—or where you *could* go—also helps you think of possibilities beyond the everyday routine.

How much more rewarding would our careers be if we embraced the process in the same way?

In this reflection, think of your career as that journey. Think of what most fulfills you. Think of your personal mission statement. Think of how you can best carry out your calling. Think about the ways you want to lead and influence others. Think about the ways you want to contribute as an individual.

This is something we can all do, even if you already feel fulfilled in your current role. All of us at Living As A Leader continue to have discussions about our next opportunities for growth and development after a quarter-century together. Recently, we've discussed how we're intrigued by the idea of providing a framework for individuals in the leadership development space to start and grow their own firms. Who knows where this will go?

Just as if you were planning a trip, you can start by daydreaming and letting your mind wander. Picture yourself in a new setting where your unique skills, talents, and traits are best utilized. Career-wise, this is your dream destination. Pay special attention to what makes you feel most fulfilled and what you can bring out in others. See yourself thriving in this role and living up to your full potential . . . and helping others do the same. What does that look like?

Next, think about what steps you need to get to this destination. Just as travel requires the planning of buying tickets, making reservations, and the time it takes to get from point A to point B, movement in your career needs the same level of deliberate attention. Think about what steps you need to take in the next days, months, or years to get to where you want to arrive.

On the following page, sketch out a road map with all the

REMEMBER TO ENJOY
THE JOURNEY.

milestones you'll need to achieve along the way to arrive. Plan your first few steps; set some goals and completion dates for yourself.

And remember to enjoy the journey.

Your Next Journey

ACKNOWLEDGMENTS

Together, we would like to thank the tens of thousands of leaders we have worked with over the past three decades. We are honored to have worked with you. You are the inspiration for this book.

Thank you to our wonderful and dedicated team at Living As A Leader—past, present, and future! It has been a privilege to work alongside you all these years. We are grateful for the work you have done to bring the concepts of *Live As A Leader* into the world of leaders.

To Tim Cigelske, an amazing writer, for being a terrific and very enjoyable co-creator of this book. Your talent for listening to people and telling their stories is magical. Without you, this book would not exist.

A special thank you to co-author John—from Aleta and Nancy—for being the painstaking detail guy on our writing team.

We are extremely grateful to our numerous clients who generously gave of their time to be interviewed for this book. Thank you so much! Your stories bring our leadership ideas and concepts to life.

We would like to thank our families, friends, and business associates for supporting us throughout the growth and evolution of our business.

And to all who are passionate about leadership effectiveness and the difference leaders make each and every day in the workplace. Effective leadership matters!

ABOUT THE AUTHORS

Aleta Norris, co-founder of Living As A Leader, has dedicated more than thirty years of her life supporting the excellence of leaders around the world. Having spent a decade, prior to co-founding Living As A Leader, affiliated with an international training firm, she has trained, coached, and developed thousands of leaders around the world. She holds a master's degree in organizational science from University of Wisconsin-Milwaukee.

Nancy Lewis, co-founder of Living As A Leader, spent several years as a training and development leader within the corporate environment. In that capacity, Nancy specialized in facilitation, program design, and providing internal consulting services. With nearly thirty-five years in the field, Nancy is highly sought after as a versatile provider to many companies within a variety of industries. She holds a master's degree in training and development, and adult education.

John Rutkiewicz joined Living As A Leader in 2012 after twenty-seven years in business serving in leadership roles. During the past two decades, he has trained and coached thousands of leaders and professionals in organizations in the U.S., Canada, Mexico, China, and the U.K. He holds a master's degree in organizational leadership and a graduate certificate in conflict mediation.

Living As A Leader Solutions

Our comprehensive leadership development program is designed to equip all leaders in your organization with the language, skill, and approach to maximize the performance and fulfillment of your employees.

Talk with us about how our team can help!

Prefer to bring leadership development into your organization yourselves? We've packaged our program so you can deliver it by certifying your own facilitators.

To learn more about Living As A Leader and our products and services, please visit livingasaleader.com.

You can also visit livingasaleaderonline.com where you'll find a number of free online resources.

Prefer a conversation? Click on the *Contact Us* button at the bottom of our website. We look forward to talking with you!

REFERENCES

Introduction

[1] Schwantes, Marcel. 2018. "Study: 60 Percent of Workers Have Quit or Are Considering Quitting Right Now. Here's the Simple Reason Why." Accessed September 25, 2020. https://www.inc.com/marcel-schwantes/why-do-people-quit-their-jobs-exactly-entire-reason-can-be-summed-up-in-1-word.html.

Chapter 1

[2] Covey, Stephen. 1998. *The 7 Habits of Highly Effective People.* Provo, UT: Franklin Covey.

[3] Glaser, Judith and Glaser, Richard. 2014. "The Neurochemistry of Positive Conversations." Accessed September 25, 2020. https://hbr.org/2014/06/the-neurochemistry-of-positive-conversations.

[4] Goleman, Daniel. 2019. "Leadership That Gets Results." Accessed September 25, 2020. https://hbr.org/2000/03/leadership-that-gets-results.

[5] Robison, Jennifer. 2006. "In Praise of Praising Your Employees." Accessed September 25, 2020. https://www.gallup.com/workplace/236951/praise-praising-employees.aspx.

6   Site staff. 2009. "How Extraordinary Leaders Double Profits." Accessed September 25, 2020. https://www.chieflearningofficer.com/2009/06/28/how-extraordinary-leaders-double-profits/.

Chapter 2

7   Adams, Linda. n.d. "Learning a New Skill is Easier Said Than Done." Accessed September 25, 2020. https://www.gordontraining.com/free-workplace-articles/learning-a-new-skill-is-easier-said-than-done/.

8   Beck, Randall and Harter, Jim. 2020. "Managers Account for 70% of Variance in Employee Engagement." Retrieved September 25, 2020. https://news.gallup.com/businessjournal/182792/managers-account-variance-employee-engagement.aspx.

Chapter 3

9   De Pree, Max. 2004. *Leadership Is An Art*, 19-20. Redfern, New South Wales: Currency.

10   Putnam, Robert D. 2000. *Bowling Alone: The Collapse and Revival of American Community.* New York: Simon & Schuster.

Chapter 4

11   Wagner, Rodd and Harter, Jim. 2007. "The First Element of Great Managing." Accessed September 25, 2020. https://news.gallup.com/businessjournal/26281/first-element-great-managing.aspx.

12 Folkman, Joseph and Zenger, John H. 2002.
    The Extraordinary Leader. New York City, NY:
    McGraw-Hill Education.

Chapter 6

13 Popper, Karl. 1999. *All Life is Problem Solving.* London
    England: Routledge.

14 Kahneman, Daniel. 2011. *Thinking, Fast and Slow.* New
    York, NY: Farrar, Strauss and Giroux.

Chapter 7

15 Lencioni, Patrick. 2012. *The Five Dysfunctions of a Team.*
    San Francisco, CA: Jossey-Bass.

Chapter 8

16 Schaeffer, Katherine. 2020. "Far more Americans see
    'very strong' partisan conflicts now than in the last two
    presidential election years." Accessed September 25, 2020.
    https://www.pewresearch.org/fact-tank/2020/03/04/far-
    more-americans-see-very-strong-partisan-conflicts-now-
    than-in-the-last-two-presidential-election-years/.

17 Smiley, Fadi. N.d. "Leadership Guide to Conflict and
    Conflict Management." Accessed September 25, 2020.
    https://ohiostate.pressbooks.pub/pubhhmp6615/chapter/
    leadership-guide-to-conflict-and-conflict-management/.

Chapter 9

18   Nicita, Camille. 2019. "Managing Change: A Mindset Of Continuous Evolution." Accessed September 25, 2020. https://www.forbes.com/sites/forbesbusinessdevelopmentcouncil/2019/07/02/managing-change-a-mindset-of-continuous-evolution/#7c85ffaf55b2.

19   Ewenstein, Boris, Smith, Wesley, and Sologar, Ashvin. 2015. "Changing change management." Accessed September 25, 2020. https://www.mckinsey.com/featured-insights/leadership/changing-change-management.

20   Bridges, Susan. 2020. "The 3 Questions." Accessed September 25, 2020. https://wmbridges.com/the-3-questions/.

21   Jellison, Jerald M. 2006. *Managing the Dynamics of Change: The Fastest Path to Creating an Engaged and Productive Workforce.* New York: McGraw-Hill.

22   Senge, Peter M. 1999. *The Dance of Change: The Challenges of Sustaining Momentum in Learning Organizations.* New York, NY: Currency/Doubleday.

23   Bridges, William and Bridges, Susan. 2016. *Managing Transitions, 25th anniversary edition: Making the Most of Change.* DeCapo Press: Boston, MA: DeCapo Press.

Chapter 10

24   Gallup. 2019. "How Millennials Want to Work and Live." Accessed September 25, 2020. https://www.gallup.com/workplace/238073/millennials-work-live.aspx.

25   Underwood, Jon. 2014. "Jon Underwood from Death Cafe on BBC World News." Accessed September 25, 2020. https://www.youtube.com/watch?v=hHk71wec198.

Chapter 11

26   Brown, Brené. 2018. *Dare to Lead: Brave Work. Tough Conversations. Whole Hearts.* United Kingdom: Ebury Digital.

Made in USA - Kendallville, IN
72519_9781647468675
03.20.2023 1330